The Book of Digital Marketing
for Plumbing & HVAC Contractors

Written by Ryan Redding

Published by DP Marketing.Services
Tulsa, Oklahoma
dpmarketing.services

ISBN: 9781731205346

Let's do this.

CONTENTS

FOREWORD

My dad was a great businessman. During the 1980s and 1990s, he hung his shingle as a pest control guy in his hometown, and he drummed up business by going door to door and taking ads in the phone book. His company never became super-massive; at its peak, he had three exterminators working for him, plus a lady answering the phone part-time. But, for a while, he was at least able to keep the company afloat, provide for his family, and get a small but loyal group of customers to vouch for his reputation.

But then the internet happened. It seemed like overnight, people were sending emails instead of sending letters, using Google instead of phone books, and using Facebook instead of talking face to face. Suddenly, the big companies in town weren't competing using the old methods that worked before. All of a sudden, the battle for customers went online. My dad's business, like hundreds of thousands of others, struggled to adapt to using the internet to find and create new customers, and eventually he had to get out of it. Sadly, I've found that my dad is not the exception.

Maybe you're like my dad. Maybe you've run your shop for years, and you've struggled to gain the competitive advantage other companies have online. Or, maybe you're just starting out, you understand the value of digital marketing, and you want to make smart decisions for your growing business. Or, maybe you're a larger shop with 50 or more vans, and you're ready to focus on improving the efficiency of your marketing efforts to maximize your profits. No matter what your reason, I truly hope this book is helpful to you.

In fact, I guarantee that if you read this book, understand the concepts, and put them into practice in your business, your company will grow. You'll have more customers. You'll have a better reputation. And you'll have a business that can dominate your market area. Nope, this isn't a get-rich-quick scheme. This is a "make better decisions than the other guy" approach. The information in here is sourced from my experience in the industry, concepts and theory from fancy graduate schools, and tons of research. This book is basically an advanced degree in digital marketing without the tuition payments.

Read this book. Refer to it often. If you have questions, get stuck, or just want us to help you implement what you've learned, drop us a line at **info@ dpmarketing.services**. No matter what you do, get ready to be busy.

Thanks for reading.

RR

CHAPTER 1:
A BRIEF HISTORY OF DIGITAL MARKETING

By 2021, digital advertising spending in the United States is expected to be just south of $120 billion—almost half of all marketing dollars.[1] Today, that's nearly twice Mark Zuckerberg's net worth. You could purchase all of Google for less money. It's a staggering amount of cha-ching, and companies are pumping more and more money into cyberspace every year.

Why? Because that's where the customers are—for an average of 24 hours per week.[2] For those who'd rather not math, I'll do it for you: That's nearly 3.5 hours per day. *Every day.*

That doesn't mean people are no longer consuming *traditional* media, of course. Cable companies are still making money hand over fist, and no matter what anyone tries to tell you, print is actually *not* dead or even gasping for air.[3] There's still a place for radio spots, postcards, and vehicle wraps. But the world is increasingly online, and so your HVAC or plumbing company must be, too.

In short, growing your business requires a calculated, digital marketing strategy. This book will teach you why and—more importantly—*how* to do that.

How the Internet Happened

"The internet? Is that thing still around?" - Homer Simpson

To understand how digital marketing is taking over the advertising space, it's helpful to put it into context: How did the internet *itself* come into existence?

For most people, it's difficult to remember—or, for the younger folks out there, even *imagine*—life before the world wide web. But there *was* such a time, and it wasn't all that long ago. Despite the internet's infiltration into nearly every aspect of our lives, it's a relatively new development.

The general idea behind the internet—a service that could collect information and distribute it to individuals around the world—is credited to Nikola Tesla in the early 1900s.[4] Then, in the 1930s and 1940s, entrepreneurs and engineers began talking about searchable storage of books.[5] Two short decades later, experimental psychologist and computer scientist J.C.R. Licklider began writing about a "universal network":

> *It seems reasonable to envision, for a time 10 or 15 years hence, a "thinking center" that will incorporate the functions of present-day libraries together with anticipated advances in information storage and retrieval.*
>
> *The picture readily enlarges itself into a network of such centers, connected to one another by wide-band communication lines and to individual users by leased-wire services. In such a system, the speed of the computers would be balanced, and the cost of the gigantic memories and the sophisticated programs would be divided by the number of users.[6]*

Around the same time that Linklider was dreaming big dreams, an American engineer and a British computer scientist were working independently on a data communications process that came to be known as "packet switching."[7] Packet switching made possible the Advanced Research Projects Agency Network (ARPANET) in the late 1960s, which was the first time several computers were linked together in a single network.[8] Then, in the 1970s, Transmission Control Protocol and Internet Protocol (TCP/IP) came about, a system that allowed multiple networks of multiple computers to talk to one another—which became the internet we know and love.[9]

Finally, in 1990, British computer scientist, Sir Tim Berners-Lee, developed the World Wide Web, which is basically the internet's "skin"— the part we see and interact with as consumers. He also created Hypertext Markup Language (HTML), Hypertext Transfer Protocol (HTTP), and a slew of other technologies[10] that changed, well, *everything*: how data is stored and recalled, the ways we communicate with one another, the pace of information sharing, access to knowledge (and, therefore, power), a whole new category of criminal activity and a need to protect ourselves from it, and on and on.

Since Berners-Lee published the very first website in 1991, digital technology for consumers has progressed at a mind-blowing clip. Since then—in just more than a quarter-century—digital technology has gone from being intellectually and physically accessible only to engineers and computer scientists to being an invited guest that's taken up permanent residence on our kitchen counters and in our back pockets. We feel naked when we leave our cell phones at home. We get irritated when Alexa doesn't understand us the first time. We ask Siri to tell us jokes. When our internet's down, we feel cranky and disconnected.

So what's the point? Well, at the risk of sounding like someone's crotchety old grandpa, here's the point: Digital technology is taking over the world. Correction: Digital technology has *already* taken over the world—quickly. And that has serious implications for your plumbing or HVAC company.

TIMELINE: THE DEVELOPMENT OF DIGITAL TECHNOLOGY

1991
World's first website is published: http://info.cern.ch/hypertext/www/TheProject.html.

1992
The first smartphone, the Simon Personal Computer, is launched.

Early precursors to Google arrive on the scene: World Wide Web Wanderer (Wandex), Archie-Like Indexing of the Web (ALIWEB), JumpStation, World Wide Web Worm, and Repository-Based Software Engineering (RBSE) spider. In the years following, several directories come online: Yahoo! Directory, Open Directory Project, Business.com, LookSmart, WebCrawler, AltaVista, and Ask Jeeves (now Ask.com) to name just a few.

1993

3

How the Digital Revolution Has Changed the Marketing Landscape

To run a successful HVAC or plumbing shop requires a good bit of grit, persistence, and hustle. You work long hours, you watch your bottom line like a hawk, and you sweat the small stuff, no matter who tells you not to. And you—more than the big guys, even—know how important it is to keep your eye on the ball, paying attention to industry trends, changing regulations, and all the other things that could sink your company in a couple of bad quarters.

One of those "other things" that could make your business a statistic is one of the most common reasons contractor businesses fail:[11] mismanagement of your marketing budget. (Have you ever stopped to realize that making dumb marketing decisions can actually cause your company to fail faster?)

The first step toward getting your arms around your ad spend is to shift most of it to the digital space. But that doesn't solve everything. It's

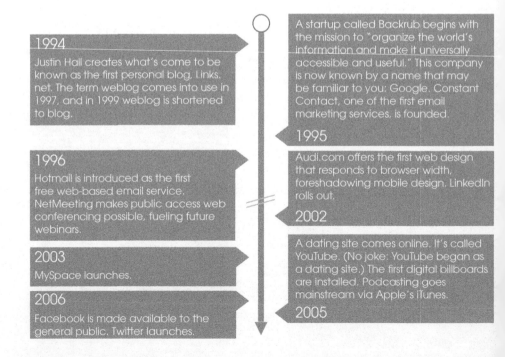

1994

Justin Hall creates what's come to be known as the first personal blog, Links. net. The term weblog comes into use in 1997, and in 1999 weblog is shortened to blog.

A startup called Backrub begins with the mission to "organize the world's information and make it universally accessible and useful." This company is now known by a name that may be familiar to you: Google. Constant Contact, one of the first email marketing services, is founded.

1995

1996

Hotmail is introduced as the first free web-based email service. NetMeeting makes public access web conferencing possible, fueling future webinars.

Audi.com offers the first web design that responds to browser width, foreshadowing mobile design. LinkedIn rolls out.

2002

2003

MySpace launches.

A dating site comes online. It's called YouTube. (No joke: YouTube began as a dating site.) The first digital billboards are installed. Podcasting goes mainstream via Apple's iTunes.

2005

2006

Facebook is made available to the general public. Twitter launches.

just as easy to waste money on digital marketing as it is on traditional marketing—unless you deal appropriately with some tough realities.

From Passive Consumers to Active Participants

As long as there have been small businesses, all the way back to ancient civilizations, there's been advertising.[12] Of course, until relatively recently, small businesses haven't had much choice beyond knocking on front doors (or hanging flyers from them), taking out yellow page ads, making cold calls, and spending a nauseating amount of money on billboards and mailing lists.

That began to change in the 20th century as innovations in entertainment and communication—radio, television, and the early days of the internet—added new opportunities to spend (and waste) precious advertising budgets. But while our marketing *methods* may have changed over time, our marketing *messages*, for the most part, simply didn't. Unless our potential customers answered their front door, picked up their phone, or responded to an email, they were still passive recipients of our messages,

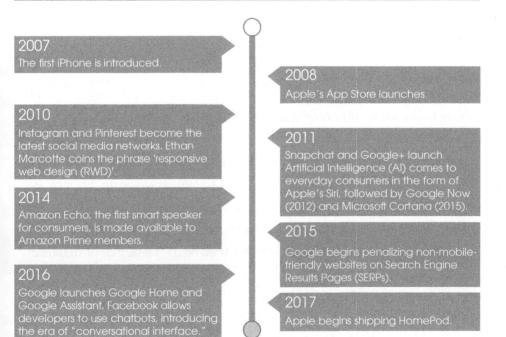

2007
The first iPhone is introduced.

2008
Apple's App Store launches.

2010
Instagram and Pinterest become the latest social media networks. Ethan Marcotte coins the phrase 'responsive web design (RWD)'.

2011
Snapchat and Google+ launch. Artificial Intelligence (AI) comes to everyday consumers in the form of Apple's Siri, followed by Google Now (2012) and Microsoft Cortana (2015).

2014
Amazon Echo, the first smart speaker for consumers, is made available to Amazon Prime members.

2015
Google begins penalizing non-mobile-friendly websites on Search Engine Results Pages (SERPs).

2016
Google launches Google Home and Google Assistant. Facebook allows developers to use chatbots, introducing the era of "conversational interface."

2017
Apple begins shipping HomePod.

and our marketing strategies reflected that. We talked *at* them, hoping they were listening.

Then came a seismic shift, and the marketing world flipped completely upside down. New technology took the power away from businesses, and handed it over to our potential customers. No longer content to simply listen as passive consumers, they're now active participants, controlling their own flow of messaging.

They zip through commercials, thanks to DVRs. They close out of banner ads and install pop-up blockers. They hit the back button on their browser when a website loads too slowly, and they gleefully unsubscribe from email marketing campaigns. They opt for paid versions of mobile apps to avoid advertisements. They check reviews and compare online prices before purchasing *anything*. And because of social media, they expect companies to hush up and *listen* for a change.

But do you know what most HVAC and plumbing companies are still doing? Strutting around talking about themselves. Using hard sales tactics. Offering coupons for services people don't even know they need. Adding a bunch of noise to people's lives and not adding anything of value or meaning.

And we wonder why our bottom line isn't getting any healthier.

Advertising in the Land of Fake News

Abraham Lincoln once said, "Don't believe everything you read on the internet." And did you know that 78% of statistics on the internet are made up? *Ahem.*

There's a lot of junk floating around on the internet, and everyone (well, most everyone) knows it. According to similarweb.com, Snopes, the "oldest and largest fact-checking site on the internet,"[13] receives more than 50 million visits per year. That's a lot of people trying to figure out if something they read or heard is actually true or if it's a bunch of malarkey.

Although fake news isn't a new concept,[14] it's a bit of cultural phenomenon these days. From what they hear on the news, in college classrooms, politicians' speeches, and town hall meetings, people are skeptical about everything.

And everything means *everything*—including you, your business ethics, your workmanship, your technicians, and your prices. People aren't going to take your word for anything anymore. There's no such thing as business over a handshake. Your potential customers have their BS meters on high alert, and they don't care what you say about your business. Know what they *do* care about? What *other* people say about your business.

Your Online Reputation

Here's how this works. If Mr. Jones' neighbor, your former customer, recommends your shop, Mr. Jones is going to hire you. Almost guaranteed. If your Google reviews are poor—particularly your star rating[15] (however unfairly or undeservedly)—*no one's* going to hire you. Again, almost guaranteed. The truth is, 68% of people form an opinion about a business after reading between one and six online reviews.[16] That's less time than it took you to read this paragraph.

Yes, people *do* care about those online reviews. Nearly 40% of consumers check reviews regularly, and 88% of people trust them as much as personal recommendations[17]—particularly if there's a mix of positive and negative comments.[18] *This is a huge deal.* The internet has made our world a smaller place, shrinking our "six degrees of separation" to just three.[19] That means people's circles of influence are vast, and we have so much less control over our reputation as a result.

Now, how about a bit of good news? Although complaints can now be expressed publicly, rather than one-on-one, research shows people are actually more likely to post a review following a *positive* experience than a negative one. What's more, one in four people have never posted a review but would consider doing so.[20] That's a huge opportunity—one we'll discuss at length in Chapter 9.

Digital Natives

The world's first website was published in 1991, which means people born that year or more recently have never lived in a world without an active world wide web. At the time of this writing, that makes more than 30% of the United States population "digital natives."[21] Sure, some of those people are infants, and not every American born after 1991 has sufficient access to technology to qualify them as digital natives. But the fact remains that most younger folks speak digital fluently, and the percentage of digital natives will obviously increase as our population ages.

Why does that matter? Because digital natives find and vet home service providers differently than their parents did. They also have different customer service expectations of the companies they hire. This makes digital marketing a *must-do*, rather than a fancy add-on.

Google is the King of Everything

Let's do some more math: Nearly 90% of American adults use the internet, up 15% from just a decade ago.[22] In 2016, Google had 246 million unique visitors in the United States.[23] That means roughly 84% of Americans who are online use Google. Sure, there are other search engines out there; but unless you have a bottomless marketing budget, it's pretty clear where you ought to be spending your ad dollars.

The Pace of Change

Back in the day, before the internet was a glimmer in a computer scientist's eye, marketing was simpler. Innovation was slow, and advertisers had a relatively limited number of channels to use. The internet and technology changed all of that.

Actually, it's more accurate to say the internet and technology *are* changing all of that. It's not as though some revolution happened and then ended. No, there's constantly something new to consider: an ever-growing list of social networks, enhanced technology like artificial intelligence (AI),

8

revised search algorithms, advanced consumer devices, and more. And since our budgets aren't necessarily growing to accommodate all the new opportunities, we have to wisely allocate our resources throughout a vast—and getting vaster—digital landscape.

The trouble, is "wise allocation" will look different next month. And the month after that. And maybe the week after that. See, it's not just that everything's changing; it's that the *pace* of change is accelerating, too. As Canadian-American journalist Graeme Wood commented, "Change has never happened this fast before, and it will never be this slow again."

If you're still following the expert digital marketing advice you heard in 2005—or even 2015—you're behind. And besides, there's really no such thing as an "expert" anymore. Some of us are paying more attention, so we're better equipped to keep up and we can be more nimble with our strategy, but what we "know" today will likely change tomorrow. It's tough to be an expert at that pace. It's exhausting, isn't it?

But your customers don't care how exhausted you are. They're overwhelmed by the pace of technological advances too,[24] but you better believe they're expecting the companies they do business with to keep up. They require convenience and customized service. They demand to be understood and to be the center of our attention. They want transparency and connection.

All of which we can provide because of technology. In the digital marketing landscape, your shop has a shot.

Digital Marketing Can Translate into Big Business for Your Small Business

The internet leveled the playing field for small businesses. As marketing guru Philip Kotler explains it:

> *The competitiveness of companies will no longer be determined by their size, country of origin, or past advantage. Smaller, younger, and locally based companies will have a chance to compete against bigger,*

older, and more global companies. Eventually, there will be no company that overly dominates the others. Instead, a company can be more competitive if it can connect with communities of customers...[25]

Marketing, when it's done well, presents your services to the right customer at the right time. Digital marketing, as complicated as it can be, makes that more possible than most traditional marketing could ever hope to.

This book will show you how.

CHAPTER 2:
YOUR TARGET CUSTOMER

Running a successful HVAC or plumbing business—or *any* small business, for that matter—involves a lot of moving parts: human resources, accounting, sales, customer service, inventory, marketing, and more. Ignoring or mishandling any of those elements can sink a business in a matter of months.

In fact, most small businesses experience a swift and painful death. After five years, only about 50% of new ventures are still afloat; five years later, another 15% have gone belly up.[1] For HVAC and plumbing companies, those numbers are even more dire, resulting in the worst failure rate of *any* industry in a five-year period.[2]

Businesses fail for multiple reasons, of course—the most obvious being a severe imbalance in their income to expense ratio. But negative account balances don't just *happen*. They're *caused*. Perhaps a service business dramatically underbid one too many jobs because they have a bad habit of undervaluing their time. Or they hired the exact wrong technician, and one unimpressed homeowner launched a negative word-of-mouth campaign. Or they lacked systems and processes to keep expenses under control. Or they too often missed converting leads to customers.

To be fair, some things are beyond your control. Natural disasters, political agendas, and severe market swings can knock you off your feet, regardless of how thoughtful and strategic your business plan might be. Recognizing that reality should compel you to be even *more* intentional with what you *can* control.

While there's no magic pill to guarantee business success, there's a secret sauce for maximizing your chances of making it past your first two years—and thriving well into the future.

The Secret Sauce:
Being an Expert On Your Customers

Obviously, your shop wouldn't exist—and won't exist for long—without customers. While it's important to know everything there is to know about your trade, it's equally important to be an expert on your customers. You need to "get" them—not just what they need from you, but also what they *want* from you.

Now, let's be clear: It's not until something goes *wrong* that someone becomes your potential customer. Whether their sewer's backed up or their air conditioning has called it quits or they need upgraded units for their business, they have a *problem.*

- For your business to thrive, you need to *solve* their problem.
- To truly solve their problem, you'll need to correctly identify your *ideal* customer base.
- To do that, you have to *understand* your ideal customer base.

When your customer picks up the phone, what are they thinking? What are they *feeling*? What's motivating them in the current moment? What are their fears? How can you move them from a potential customer to an *actual* customer?

How Your Customers Make Decisions

Believe it or not, people make decisions for only one of two reasons. That's it. Once you understand those two reasons, you'll be better equipped to meet your customers' needs and wants.

1. **Money.** People who are financially motivated are more likely to become customers if they make money or, more relevant to HVAC and plumbing problems, they *save* money. Their decision to engage your services will come down to dollars and cents. So, you're

likely to be successful with these customers if you offer incentives like coupons, rebates, and promotions. It also helps to be honest, transparent, up-front, and fair with your pricing. *Note:* That does *not* mean you have to be the least expensive shop in town.

2. **Emotions.** People who are motivated by emotion make decisions because of how something makes them feel: stronger, smarter, safer, sexier, etc. These customers tend to make subconscious, involuntary, emotionally charged decisions that often defy pure logic. In fact, they often don't know *why* they've made the choice they have, and when pressed to explain their decision, these folks may actually *change their mind.*[3]

Of course, people don't necessarily make decisions for the same reason every time. There are probably some decisions you make in your life that are motivated entirely by money—a mortgage refinance or investment choice, for example. On the other hand, you've likely made more emotional decisions; maybe you rescued a dog from a shelter, got married, or moved across the country to be nearer to family.

Let's pick a specific example we can all identify with: smartphones. Chances are, you use a smartphone nearly every day to play games, respond to email, text your team, and, from time to time, even make phone calls. Most smartphones are made up of very similar features: they have touch screens, apps for productivity and entertainment, and cameras for taking photos of your lunch.

For the bulk of the past decade, the smartphone market has been dominated by two main heavyweights: Google and Apple. Their two products, Androids and iPhones respectively, offer basically the same functions, right? But they're marketed in quite different ways.

If you go look at any store that sells Android phones—whether Pixels, Samsungs, or LGs— you'll likely see something like this:

See that? That ad's promoting a sale with an additional 5% cashback. **Money trigger.**

Now, let's look at Apple:

There's iPhone.
And then there's everything else.

What makes an iPhone unlike anything else? Maybe it's that it lets you do so many things. Or that it lets you do so many things so easily. Those are two reasons iPhone owners say they love their iPhone. But there are many others as well.

Nothing about price. Nothing about rebates. But notice what it does do: It strokes your ego that you're better than everyone else when you have an iPhone. **Emotional trigger.**

You can find examples like this everywhere. Steakhouses. Car dealerships. Clothing. People will only respond to one of those two triggers—either money or emotion. Period.

14

How does this apply to your plumbing or HVAC company? Simply put, you'll successfully reach more customers if you understand their primary decision trigger. For example, if you're heavily focused on service, chances are your customers—at least your *preferred* customers—are going to be more emotionally motivated than they are financially motivated.

Having Empathy for Your Customers

So, your customers are motivated by either money or emotion. They have a more fundamental need, too: *They want to be understood.*

Empathy, or the ability to understand another person's experience (feelings), isn't often listed among the top 10 characteristics of successful entrepreneurs. Why? Because until relatively recently, marketing has been business-focused, not customer-focused. We've spent years telling customers about *ourselves*, rather than inviting them to tell us about *themselves.*

The digital space—social media, in particular—has changed the game. Customers expect to be engaged in conversation, not talked at. What's more, people are generally pretty skeptical, and they're looking for evidence—believable, "feel-able" evidence—that a business can be trusted. Companies that yammer on and on about themselves fall to the bottom of the pile. Companies that take the time to ask questions, listen, and express some give-a-damn? Those companies *win.*

To be clear, this isn't just about social media engagement. Let's say a customer calls you with a problem. I'm guessing you've heard about and seen *everything.* From kids' toys down the toilet to birds nesting in the air conditioning compressor, it's just another day at the office for you. But to the customer asking for an estimate, it's an entirely different matter. What's routine for you is an unexpected, undesired, likely expensive, inconvenience-bordering-on-disaster for them. *And they need to know you hear them, you care about their experience, and you can do something to make it all better—without breaking the bank.*

What does this have to do with digital marketing? It may seem like the only way to express empathy toward customers is when you're having a conversation with them in person or on the phone. But empathy is more foundational than that. If you're constantly thinking about your business *from your customer's perspective* you'll change how you communicate with them—not only in person, but also online and in print.

How Empathy Can Guide Marketing Decisions

There's no shortage of advertising opportunities these days, and it's easy to waste money. By understanding your customers' mindset—by having empathy for their experiences—you'll naturally spend your marketing dollars and energy in the most advantageous direction and avoid wasting any money where it's not going to be as effective.

I mentioned earlier that emotion is a trigger for many of your customers, and research[4] has uncovered eight different emotional states that guide purchasing decisions. Two of those eight are particularly relevant to your HVAC or plumbing company.

Needs Validation

Customers in this emotional state need to know they're making the *right* decision, and they value others' opinions. How can you show them you're the right shop to meet their needs? What marketing strategies best resonate with this emotional state? Online reviews, interaction on social media, and expert advice will address customers' concerns about making the wrong choice.

Decision Anxiety

Some customers get overwhelmed not because they're afraid of making the wrong decision, but simply because there are too many options. By optimizing your website for search and by investing in Google Ads or Google Local Services, your business will rise to the top of search results,

16

rather than floating somewhere in the middle of "too many choices." In fact, Google itself recently acted on this by changing their map-pack listing from seven companies down to only three. (See Chapters 6 and 7 for more on all things Google.)

By the way, given that it's more expensive to gain new business than it is to keep current customers,[5] it's helpful to remember that some people experience decision anxiety even *after* they've already made their choice. Maintaining a connection after your work is complete (i.e., continuing to "market" to people whom you've already served) can confirm to anxious customers that they made the right decision in hiring you:

> *By inviting engagement throughout the customer experience journey [before, during, and after a sale], we can develop relationship-based loyalty, rather than the more fickle transaction-based version.*[6]

Being Human

Really, what all of this empathy stuff comes down to is remembering that, at the end of the day, your business is made up of human beings dealing with other human beings. And this isn't just touchy-feely mumbo-jumbo from a tender-hearted marketing guy; this is an actual business practice known as *human-centric marketing*.[7]

Four attributes of human-centric marketing are particularly helpful for plumbing and HVAC companies:

- **Sociability.** Companies with good sociability display excellent verbal and nonverbal communication skills. Listening well, engaging in conversations, resolving differences, and sharing meaningful information are helpful to fostering relationships— including business relationships. Having an active social media presence offers all sorts of opportunities for you to interact with your potential customers in meaningful ways—one-on-one. (See Chapter 8 for more on this.)

- **Emotionality.** We've talked about emotion quite a bit already, but it bears repeating that companies who can connect with people on an emotional level will earn customers. Empathizing with people's frustration when they have a plumbing or HVAC problem is important, but so is showing your human side through inspiration and even humor.

- **Personability.** Another word for personability is *authenticity*. Plumbing and HVAC shops with personability are *real*. They know what they're good at, and they're not afraid to admit when they've made a mistake. For example, if a customer were to post an unfavorable review on Facebook, they wouldn't get defensive or simply ignore the criticism; they'd address it carefully and compassionately.

- **Morality.** Given that many of your potential customers are just *certain* you're going to rip them off, fine-tuning this aspect of human-centric marketing is particularly important. People want to know your values, and they want assurance that you're an ethical company.

In short, authenticity about who you are as a person and transparency about who you are as a business will go a long way toward gaining trust—which will earn you more customers.

The Difference Between Install and Service Customers

Obviously, not all of your customers are seeking help in emergency situations. You also have an opportunity to serve homeowners and businesses who are replacing, remodeling, or upgrading equipment and fixtures.

Without question, install customers are also concerned about being taken advantage of. But they have a significant leg up over your leads with a dead furnace during a blizzard or an uncooperative toilet an hour before the in-laws arrive. They have *time*.

Prospective install clients will take all the time they need to thoroughly vet contractors. Sure, it's still important to have a disarming, mobile-friendly website that appears "above the fold" on a search engine results page (SERP). But you can't stop there. These customers aren't just looking for *someone* to fix their problem; they're looking for a bona fide *expert* to fix their problem.

Yes, expertise is important to service clients, too. Of course it is. But those customers are more concerned about *fast*. Most installation customers *also* have a timeline, but they're more willing to extend it to find the exact right shop for their job.

So how do you show *install* customers you're the best choice? By publishing (free) expert content; having loads of authentic, complimentary reviews; getting trackbacks to your website, and more. We'll get to all of that later in the book.

For now, here's the most important takeaway—for both service and install customers: **Get outside yourself and your business goals and objectives, and think about what it's like to be the customer reaching out for help.** Then treat them how you'd hope to be treated.

Just like your momma taught you.

CASE STUDY

*In this book, I'll be throwing a ton of information at you, and I understand it can be tough to really grasp the concepts without seeing some real-world examples. So, I've put together some case studies based on actual data from actual clients whom I've helped put this stuff into practice. You'll find those case studies online at **dpmarketing.services/game-changer**. Here's our first one:*

Taggart Plumbing wanted to raise money for folks affected by Hurricane Florence. They set a generous goal and tackled it through a savvy omni-channel marketing campaign. Visit **dpmarketing.services/game-changer** to see what happens when contractors show they care about the community.

YOUR NEXT STEPS

Often, the first place your customers will encounter your company is on the internet. So, conduct an "empathy" audit of your website, by asking the following questions:

- ❐ When a potential customer lands on your homepage, will they think, "This company 'gets' me and my problem"?

- ❐ Does your site address those two decision triggers: money and emotion?

- ❐ Can customers easily navigate your site? Have you removed every possible obstacle to them finding what they need?

- ❐ Do you have a hassle-free way for people to reach you?

- ❐ Is your website mobile-friendly? (No one wants to deal with an antiquated website when they're in an HVAC or plumbing crisis.)

- ❐ Have you established your expertise through testimonials, reviews, or mentions of awards you've earned?

- ❐ Is your copy authentic? Disarming, even? (See the sidebar on page 26 for an example.)

CHAPTER 3:
YOUR DIGITAL MARKETING PLAN

Successful marketing comes down to two things: persistence and intentionality. And really, it's the *combination of the two* that makes the difference.

- You could stubbornly continue to place an ad in the yellow pages year after year after year. That's persistent, but not intentional. (Seriously, guys: When was the last time you used the Yellow Pages for anything but a booster seat at the kids' table on Thanksgiving?)

- You could do a one-day Google Ads blitz. That's intentional, but not persistent. Pay per click (PPC) ad campaigns are a definite must-have in your digital strategy—particularly as you're trying to boost your website ranking—but they aren't a one-day deal.

Don't get me wrong, you might get lucky with a random, one-off advertisement at some point in your company's history—but you'll likely waste a bunch of money along the way. You don't rely on luck in any other area of your business, right? Do you bring on new technicians without an interview and just *cross your fingers* that they know what they're doing? Do you buy parts without price-checking and just *hope* you're getting a great deal? Of course not. You're careful about how and when you spend every dime for your shop. Why would you be all willy-nilly with your marketing dollars?

That's right: You wouldn't be. Or, if you have been, you won't be anymore. You need a plan.

The Foundations of a Digital Marketing Plan

On a foundational level, your digital marketing plan has two major components: the methods you use to reach people (the what) and the people you're trying to reach (the who). Let's quickly unpack each of those elements.

The What: Omni-Channel Marketing

Our customers are unique individuals, which means there's no such thing as one formula that will bring you success in every situation with every potential customer. That means you need a diversified, or *omni-channel*, marketing strategy. Please understand that *diversified* is not code for *scattershot*. Yes, you'll be connecting with potential customers through many different media, but your efforts will still be *coordinated* and *purposeful*.

This approach takes a little more forethought and energy, but it actually takes less time and money because you'll get to re-purpose your marketing content across multiple channels. Plus, you'll get to take advantage of three different types of media: paid, earned, and owned.

Owned Media are the channels that belong to you and over which you have complete control of outbound messaging. This includes your website, blog, and the space you occupy on social media. Of course, the less authority you assume over those last two, the less you "own" them. If, for example, you allow unmediated blog comments or you let people post publicly to your Facebook Page, that content becomes earned media, which I'll get to in a moment.

Paid Media is precisely what it sounds like: the marketing on which you spend money. Both traditional and digital advertising lands here, such as TV spots and Google Ads, direct mailers and social media boosts.

Earned Media is where digital marketing really sings and, you'll be pleased to know, costs you nothing (other than the remarkable customer service you offer to get it). Earned media includes reviews and recommendations, shares, blog comments, word of mouth referrals, and so on. It's advertising that other people do on your behalf *because you earned it*. *Note:* Earned media is not always positive. If people start dropping negative reviews on Google, whether or not it feels "fair," you, unfortunately, "earned" those single-star ratings. You'll learn how to navigate that in Chapter 9.

The Who: The Conversion Funnel

Humor me for a moment, and imagine a funnel. A *large* funnel. It doesn't matter what color it is, what it's made of, or if it's the one in your kitchen or your garage. It just needs to be funnel-shaped: a wide opening at the top that gets progressively narrower as you move toward the bottom.

Next, apply a sticker with your company logo to the side of your imaginary funnel, and then fill it up with people. (I told you it needed to be large, didn't I?) All of those people inside your funnel—every one of them—is either a prospective customer or they've turned into (converted to) a *customer*-customer. Your funnel is wide at the top because you have way more prospects than you do qualified leads, and you have far more qualified leads than you do actual customers. You follow?

Oh, and one more thing. Add some folks *beneath* the funnel, and picture them shouting accolades up to the people still making their way through. They could also be talking to their neighbors or posting on Google or Facebook. Those folks? They're your *brand advocates,* and they're super important. I'll talk about that a bit later.

Another way to think about the conversion funnel is **your customer's path to purchase**. It's how your potential customers go from:

- knowing zilch about your HVAC or plumbing shop

- to knowing you exist

- to deciding you're the right people for the job

- to telling everyone they know how terrific you are.

Fortunately, the conversion funnel is reasonably predictable, and if you're intentional and smart, there are ways to help people navigate the process better. Plus—and you'll love this one—it doesn't require you to be all up in people's faces all the time, spamming them with advertisements and cold calls. Instead, you only need to present certain messages to certain customers—based on their position in the funnel.

If you Google *conversion funnel, marketing funnel,* or *customer path to purchase,* you'll see multiple variations on a theme, many of which dive into the history and evolution of the original funnel concept. Some even suggest the funnel isn't really funnel-shaped at all; it's more like an hourglass or a bow tie. It's a bit overwhelming, honestly, so I'm going to cut to the chase and teach you just one version—one that's been highly successful for HVAC and plumbing shops.

- Awareness
- Interest
- Preference
- Conversion
- Advocacy

To make this more practical, let's squish those five funnel touchpoints into three major stages: Top of the Funnel (TOFU), Middle of the Funnel (MOFU), and Bottom of the Funnel (BOFU).

Meeting Your Customers Where They Are

In general, your customers will move through three stages in the funnel:

- **TOFU: Awareness.** In this stage, you're letting people know you exist and that you have some connection to their problem. Potential customers at the top of the funnel say about your company, "I've heard of you."

- **MOFU: Interest and Preference.** In the middle of the funnel, you pique people's interest in who you are and what you know, and then you help guide them toward choosing you as a solution to their problem. In the middle of the funnel, customers say, "I'm interested—but only from afar" and then, if you're successful in drawing them toward you, "I'm convinced you're the company to help me."

- **BOFU: Conversion and Advocacy.** At the bottom of the funnel, dollars exchange hands and your thrilled customers begin to market your shop for you. (Sounds great, doesn't it? It works. You'll see.) Here, customers say about you, "Take my money," and "I'm going to tell everyone I know about you!"

Let's get specific about how to engage your customers at each phase of the funnel.

TOFU Digital Marketing Strategy: Build Awareness

At the top of the conversion funnel, your primary job is to make sure people know you exist. That may not seem like a terribly complex goal until you consider people hear or see between 4,000 and 10,000 marketing messages per day.[1] In addition to competing for attention

A FUNNEL EXAMPLE: Spokes

Spokes is a bicycle shop in the suburban Midwest. They have plenty of competition, including a big box sports store, two major discount stores that sell less expensive bikes and parts, and another specialty cycling store run by a beloved family in their community.

Still, Spokes has managed to survive their first five years in business, and they're becoming known for their unmatched, "surprise and delight" approach to customer service. They'd like to grow their business to the point that they can open a second shop in a nearby community.

inside all that noise, we're competing with time. Research suggests that people "experience the world in 3-second time frames."[2] Hugs last an average of three seconds. Musical phrases are about three seconds long. Babies babble in three-second bursts.

Stokes'
TOFU STRATEGY

Our friends at Spokes have tried all sorts of traditional marketing, including postcards to new residents, billboards, and an ad in their community magazine's annual "get outside" edition. Mostly, they feel like they're blowing their ad budget on things they can't measure.

A couple of weeks ago, they participated in their town's health fair because they know customers appreciate businesses that are involved in the community. (Fortunately for Spokes, their competitors didn't bother with the fair.)

One person, Alex, approached their booth primarily for the free granola bar, but after talking with one of the sales people, she remembered seeing a clever advertisement Spokes had run. Although she'd been saving up for a new road bike, she had a long way to go and really hadn't settled on anything specific. She took a coupon just to be nice and went on her way.

What does that mean for your HVAC or plumbing marketing plan? It means you have a whopping three seconds to battle through as many as 10,000 marketing messages. Yikes. That's why relying on one kind of marketing from one channel *will not work*.

For plumbing and HVAC shops, your TOFU strategy should involve two main tactics: traditional advertising and a great website.

Traditional Advertising

Traditional advertising tends to be both expensive and "ready-fire-aim." In other words, most of the folks who accidentally hear about you through traditional advertising tactics aren't *remotely* interested in what you have to offer. Practically speaking, that means a low return on investment (ROI).

To prove the point, when was the last time you drove past a billboard and then picked up your cell phone to buy whatever they were promoting?

Even if a billboard really caught your attention—it was clever or had a catchy URL you were certain you'd never forget—by the time you could investigate further, you'd likely forgotten all about it.

Still, it can be smart to integrate traditional and digital marketing. Just be aware of what you're really getting in terms of conversion rates for HVAC and plumbing businesses, specifically:

- Direct mailers: 25:1 (for current customers)

- Door hangers: 50:1 (for prospects)

- Billboards: 10,000 to 1

By comparison, the conversion rate for Google Ads is 9:1 for well-managed accounts, and referrals generate conversions at roughly 1:1.

Your Website

Your website should introduce people to your plumbing or HVAC business at the exact right time: when they have a problem you were born to solve. For TOFU prospective customers, your website must be optimized for search and must be mobile responsive. Chapters 6 and 7 tackle the why and how of both.

MOFU Digital Marketing Strategy: Drive Interest and Win Preference

People in the middle of the funnel are, at first, only peripherally interested in your company. But then, because of your efforts, they come to *prefer* you over the competition.

Here's a for-instance: My kids—like most kids—like to eat. We have a Whataburger a mile from my driveway, but my kids would rather wait a few extra minutes—even when they're staaaaaarving, Daaaaaaaad!—while I drive them to the McDonald's five miles away. They simply prefer Mickey D's, and their preference strongly influences where my dollars end up.

Spokes'
MOFU STRATEGY

Spokes recently hired a copywriter to do some blogging for them, which they've been able to repurpose as content for their Facebook Page. Since they're intentional about doing customer-oriented (not business-oriented) blog posts, they've started to get more likes and follows on social media. Plus, their recent posts, "Top 10 Bike Trails in Smithton" and "Microbrews Within Biking Distance," earned them backlinks from other local businesses—which boosted their Google ranking nicely.

In the last couple of weeks, a few new customers have stopped by with the coupons they distributed at the health fair, and the reusable straws they had imprinted with their website were a huge hit at the last Chamber of Commerce event. Alex, from the fair, happened upon Spokes' microbrews post when one of her favorite breweries, who made the list, shared it on their own Facebook Page. She followed the link to Spokes' Page and liked it—in case she ever managed to save up enough money for an upgraded bike. She checked the expiration date on the coupon, then stuck it on the fridge door.

Moving prospective customers past awareness and to interest and preference is the trickiest part of the whole funnel. Your prospective customers need to discover two things:

1. You know what you're talking about.

2. You can solve their problem.

HVAC and plumbing shops can be most effective at engaging mid-funnel customers by using content marketing, call centers (or the equivalent), peer-to-peer conversion, and swag.

Content Marketing

A 2016 study showed that 76% of business-to-consumer companies in North America used content marketing and invested more than a quarter of their marketing budget to do so.[3] I tell you that because when I explain what content marketing is, you may think I made it up. I didn't. It's been around since Benjamin Franklin published his first *Poor Richard's Almanack* (although to be fair it only caught on significantly this century).[4]

This is going to seem a bit backward, but it's a foundational principle of the conversion funnel. Ready? Here goes: The gist of content marketing is giving prospective customers your stuff—your expertise, knowledge, and advice—for free. Yes, for free. For example, rather than pitching your HVAC preventive maintenance program, you teach people how to do their *own* preventive maintenance. Or rather than pushing your after-hours drain clean-out services, you provide blog posts with detailed instructions for homeowners to clear their *own* clogs.

Now, before you slam this book closed and demand a refund, take a deep breath and let's talk through this a bit.

As we've already established, people are tired of listening to companies talk about themselves. So when HVAC and plumbing companies offer valuable content that's relevant to people's lives—with no strings attached—they sit up and take notice.

I know your fear is that if people go all DIY on everything you'll never get any paying customers. But here's what *actually* happens: People will still call you to do the things you've taught them to do themselves. People don't *want* to clean their own drains and ducts. They just want to know the company they've hired to do those things is a *good company.* Content marketing is one way to show them.

At this stage of the funnel, content marketing is also a critical component of search engine optimization (SEO). Plus, a well-developed content strategy gives you something to share on your social channels—

something more (and better) than yet another coupon or sales announcement or whatever you're currently posting that's being completely ignored.

Call Centers (and Equivalent)

These days, people are accustomed to getting the information they need *right now*. Since a good number of people still make actual phone calls,[5] it's a good idea to have a **clickable/tappable "Call now!" button on your website**. Just be sure that phone number is always answered by a human being, not a machine. Promptly. Even (or especially) at 3 am.

Now let's move the call center idea into the digital age.

- While 43% of people will pick up a phone to connect with a company, 73% of them are happier doing so using live chat.[6]
- Fifty-one percent of people want 24/7 accessibility to businesses, nearly 46% would rather message a company than send an email, and 49% want to communicate with a business through messages *before calling them*.[7]

If you're feeling discouraged because giving customers 24/7 access sounds complicated and expensive, I have good news for you: Facebook is now offering a Messenger integration for business websites.[8] That means your HVAC or plumbing company can tap into the power of Messenger (which 1.2 billion people were using as of April 2017[9]) and all of its techy goodness: chatbots, payments, photos, and videos. It also means people can continue their conversation with you directly from Facebook Messenger, rather than having to stay put on your website. That is truly *on-demand* consumer service—both *convenient* and *human-centric*.

Peer-to-Peer Conversion

MOFU prospective customers move from interest to preference for a handful of reasons, but getting a thumbs up from another human being—

someone other than you or someone who works for you—is the most significant one. As I've said before, your prospective customers don't care what *you* say about you; they only care about what *other people* say about you. It's really helpful, therefore, to get reviews, recommendations, and testimonials out in front of people. Hold that thought until Chapter 9.

Swag

Swag is any giveaway on which you've put your company's information: pens, t-shirts, stickers, reusable bags, thumb drives, and so on. You're right: These things are not "digital marketing," but they serve two purposes in the MOFU. They *point* to your digital channels and they say something about your company values. That means whatever you're giving away should have your website address on it—and preferably a unique landing page with its own URL so you can target your messaging and track ROI. It also means your swag better be *good*. If you're giving any junk, *that's* what people will think of your values.

BOFU Digital Marketing Strategy: Convert Sales and Create Advocates

Moving prospective customers from TOFU through MOFU all the way down to BOFU is how your HVAC or plumbing shop stays alive. MOFU folks *prefer* you, but they'll only use you if and when they have a problem and only if you can solve their exact problem exactly when they need you to. So, preference is good. *Conversion*—getting a new customer—is obviously your goal.

But the *real* magic happens at the advocacy touchpoint. Your new customer, who has handed you actual money, will now begin to hand you additional customers. You've done a fantastic job moving them through the funnel, and because your services were expertly rendered, fairly priced, and courteously delivered, they're quick to offer a recommendation and online review. They're now an advocate for your brand, bringing new customers to you with little additional effort on your part.

As an HVAC or plumbing company, your BOFU strategies should include PPC, unparalleled customer service, post-purchase communication, and reputation management. (In case you're wondering, managing your reputation has a huge influence on that 1:1 conversion rate from personal recommendations I mentioned earlier.)

Notice I did *not* list social media among your BOFU strategies. Many companies make the mistake of thinking Facebook's going to bring them qualified leads just itching to convert. While that may be true in some retail contexts, it only rarely happens in the service industry. That doesn't mean plumbing and HVAC companies won't benefit from a healthy social presence, of course. I'll say lots more about this in Chapter 8.

Pay Per Click Advertising (PPC)

Most "advertising" belongs toward the top and middle of the conversion funnel. PPC ads, though, are critical right here at the bottom— particularly for a customer who arrived home to a crisis HVAC or plumbing situation and dove straight to the bottom of the funnel. They have a problem, and they need a solution right now.

Chances are better than good that this frustrated, BOFU homeowner is going to pull out their phone, open the Google app, and type "plumber [your town]" or "heater repair [your town]." **If you're not among the first companies listed on the SERP, you will not win that customer.** A PPC campaign makes it more likely that you will be listed toward the top of the SERP. We'll teach you everything you need to know about PPC ads in Chapter 7.

Customer Service

I cannot overstate this, but I'm going to try, because it's that important. **If your shop sucks,** you won't get any more customers, you'll lose the ones you currently have, your dreams of retiring to a beach somewhere will never come true, you'll lose the respect of your family (including your dog), and your neighbors will TP your house every weekend until you die.

In all seriousness, if you learn nothing else from this book, I hope you'll learn (or be reminded) of this: Customer service will make or break your business. And I'm not only talking about the quality of your work; I'm also talking about the attitude with which you do it. Also, notice I haven't said anything about the *price* of your work. What matters here is how you treat people. If you do well by folks, they'll come back to you the next time—and they'll bring friends. Even if you're not the least expensive option.

Post-Purchase Communication and Reputation Management

You're done with a sale or job when someone pays your invoice. But you're not done with your customer until… well, *ever.*

- The thing about plumbing and HVAC systems is they don't last forever.
- The thing about *people* is they'll go back to the same company time and time again if they were happy with the service they received.

- The *other* thing about people is that they're nevertheless tempted to try someone else a friend recommended or to be wooed by a less expensive option.

- The thing about *marketing* is it's a good way to remind people you exist and why they love you.

So, when you've completed a job, you should *follow up:*

- Get an email address from every customer and share preventive maintenance tips with them a couple of times each year.

- Develop a customer satisfaction survey—a short one that's easy, and even fun, to complete. Model it after those goofy quizzes on Facebook that people pretend to think are dumb but do anyway. Leave a hand-written thank you card at a job site, and include the web address where your survey lives. If you don't receive feedback after three or four days, send an email to the customer, reminding them to do it. If you did good work, if you were kind, and if your reminder note is friendly and fun, they'll likely do you a favor.

- Ask customers to leave you a review on Facebook and Google, and teach them how to do it.

- Check in once or twice a year to see if you can be of any service to current customers.

- Offer loyalty discounts and maintenance agreements.

The Speed of the Funnel

For contractors, the speed with which people move through the funnel depends on if they're service customers or commercial/install customers. As you'd expect, a homeowner in a plumbing or HVAC crisis is going to zip through the funnel, relying heavily on search engine results and Google star ratings. Someone looking to upgrade equipment or a business with some time on its hands will be more methodical, exploring every nook and cranny of the funnel and requiring a good bit of nurturing.

Right-Sizing Your Expectations (and Your Budget)

Keep in mind that some potential customers require fewer touchpoints than others before they convert, and some people seem to cycle up and down through the funnel before finally dropping out the bottom. It's not *always* a linear process, in other words, and our Spokes example is certainly the *ideal* scenario.

Just try to remember there aren't many "wrong" ways to approach your digital marketing plan—although there are some plans of attack that are (unnecessarily) more expensive. In short, there are multiple variations of "right"—some, perhaps, right-er than others. My goal is to help you develop a plan that makes sense for *your* HVAC or plumbing company and that actually grows your customer base and revenue. What it comes down to, even for potential customers whose path to purchase has multiple detours, is **maximizing movement from the top to the bottom and beyond.**

YOUR NEXT STEPS

☐ If you don't already have one, develop (or purchase) a customer relationship management system (CRM) that will allow you to keep track of potential, current, and former customers and how you engage with them over time. Admittedly, it's a bit of a headache to get your CRM going at first—but the headache is worth it. A good CRM is an invaluable tool for automating sales and post-sales processes—which you'll definitely need to do as you experience success with your digital marketing strategy.

☐ Make a list of all the marketing collateral you already have in each part of the funnel: TOFU, MOFU, and BOFU. Think through how you could repurpose certain pieces of content for different touchpoints. What are the gaps you need to cover?

☐ Brainstorm a list of *new* TOFU, MOFU, and BOFU marketing strategies you'd like to try.

☐ Draft up a post-purchase communication plan. How will you keep your happy customers in your pipeline?

CHAPTER 4:
FROM WHAT TO HOW

At this point, you may be thinking, "All right, already! Digital marketing is important! I get it! I even know what PPC means. Now tell me how to actually *do* it."

Perfect. I'm glad you're feeling that way, because we've reached that point in the book—the point at which we move away from the "what" and "why" and straight into "how." This is when the fun happens. You're about to learn how to:

- speak Google

- make immediate changes to your website to get more business

- use social media to your benefit

- build major street cred in your community

- know if anything you're doing is actually working

Fair warning: For the next few chapters, we're heading for the weeds, friends. To avoid wasting money trying to grow your business, it's critical to pay attention to all of the details. Fortunately, although digital marketing is a good mix of science and art, it's mostly science. That means very few of the details are arbitrary. Digital marketing is (or should be) a data-driven decision-making process. I'm going to teach you what that looks like. Along the way, you'll see some words, phrases, and acronyms that may be unfamiliar to you. If you get stuck, you'll find a glossary in the appendix.

Before I head to the weeds, how about I answer the question that's likely been in the back of your mind since you cracked open this book: How much is this digital marketing stuff going to cost me?

Your Digital Marketing Budget

You can spend very little money on marketing and experience a little bit of a return. You can also spend a whole, whole lot of money—and experience that same little bit of return. The key is to set a reasonable and realistic budget and then allocate those dollars well—in the places that are most likely to bring you more customers.

According to the Small Business Association (SBA), your overall marketing budget should be 7-8% of your annual revenue. If you spend less than that, you'll struggle to have sufficient inbound leads to stay afloat. In other words using 7-8% of your revenue for marketing will keep your business level consistent.

Now, if you want to *grow* your business, you may need to be prepared to invest anywhere from 9% to 15% on your marketing. If you go this route, be sure your shop can handle the increased number of leads you'll get from an effectively boosted marketing budget. Otherwise, your customer service will be negatively affected, which will negatively affect your bottom line.

Finally (and this should be obvious) if you're spending more than 10% of your revenue on marketing and you're struggling to get enough inbound leads to keep your shop stable, there's a *quality of marketing* problem.

So how much of that 7-8% budget should be allocated to digital channels vs. traditional/mass media? A big chunk of it. Without knowing the specifics of your shop, your current revenue, and your potential revenue, it's tough to offer a more specific answer than that.

To give you an idea, data shows that companies are now spending just over 40% of their overall marketing budget online, up from 29% in 2014. The most popular tactics are Search Engine Marketing (SEM) (both paid and organic), display ads (including video), and social media ads.[1]

YOUR NEXT STEPS

☐ Determine what your monthly marketing budget is currently.

☐ Determine what your monthly marketing budget should be:

  ○ Write down your average annual revenue.

  ○ Multiply that number by .08 (or 8%) to see what your overall marketing budget should be.

  ○ Now, divide that number by 12. That's your target monthly advertising spend.

According to the formula, if you're a $900,000 shop, your total marketing budget should be around $72,000 per year, and your digital marketing budget should be at least $28,800 per year (though your mileage may vary).

That's a lot of money to throw into the wind, eh? So let's not do that. Over the next few chapters, you'll learn how to spend it on purpose instead.

CHAPTER 5:
WEBSITE USER EXPERIENCE (UX) AND CONTENT

These days, when people need help with anything—the name of a song, ideas for birthday gifts, or someone to come deal with a burst pipe or an uncooperative furnace—they turn to the internet. In fact, some studies suggest that as many as 97% of people research local service companies online. If people aren't finding your website, or if your website isn't helpful to them, you'll very likely lose them as potential customers.

So, if you want to grow your HVAC or plumbing business, you need a good website. What, exactly, does it mean to have a "good" website? In short, **it means it does its job: converts leads into customers.** The ins and outs of how to best accomplish that are complex, for sure, but all the tactics boil down to two things:

- Google has to know about your website and deem it worthy of showing to potential customers.

- Potential customers have to know within about 10 seconds[1] of landing on your site if you're the solution to their problem.

If you follow the practical suggestions in the next three chapters, your website *will* rank higher on search results, *will* bring you more potential customers, and *will* convert leads. To be honest, it's a ton of work—but few things worth doing are easy, right? (And remember: If you see an unfamiliar word or acronym along the way, refer to the glossary you'll find in the Appendix.)

In Chapters 6 and 7, you'll learn how Google finds your website, and that's obviously critical to your digital marketing plan. **But ultimately your website isn't made for Google; it's made for people**—people whom you hope will become your customers. So let's talk about that first. What are some critical components of human-friendly websites? (Oh, and in case you're wondering: Yes, having a human-friendly website actually makes Google happy, too.)

Mobile Responsiveness

Having a mobile-friendly website isn't a technical tactic; it's an empathic one. Right now, more than 52% of web traffic happens from mobile devices,[2] and the desktop-to-mobile margin is expected to widen. If your customer comes home during a record-setting heat wave to an air conditioner that's gone kaput, they don't need the additional frustration of having to deal with your antiquated website. So they *won't* deal with that frustration; they'll move on to your competitor.

Listen, at least half of your potential customers are likely looking at your website on an itty bitty screen, and your site should respond accordingly. That means regardless of the device people are using, they shouldn't have to scroll left and right to see the entire page, the navigation menu should always be visible, and the copy should be legible without pinching and dragging to enlarge it. If any of those three things doesn't work well, your potential customers will hit the back button in a heartbeat and go find one of your competitors to give their money to instead.

Finally, while I know I said just a couple of paragraphs ago that this section is about people, I do need to mention one Google-y thing. Our search engine friend is now not only *penalizing* non-mobile sites on SERP rankings,[3] but also it's using mobile sites as the *starting point* for SERP rank.[4] It'll still index your desktop site, but if your mobile experience is poor or nonexistent, you'll get dinged.

Readability

No one wants to read poorly written content—whether it's dull, overly complicated, full of grammatical errors, or stuffed with keywords. Your prospective customers will appreciate a well-written, simple-to-understand website that seems to "get" them. Yes, human-centric marketing definitely applies to the words on your website.

Google agrees. In fact, in early 2017, Google's Webmaster Trends Analyst Gary Illyes tweeted, "... if you read out loud the text on your page and it doesn't sound natural, that piece of text may weigh much less during ranking."[5] Although it's unlikely Google is actively grading anyone's prose, readability certainly affects how long users will stay on a site and how often they'll return, and those factors *do* affect SERP rank.

For websites, readability largely comes down to the length of sentences and paragraphs. I hate to break it to you, but no one's coming to your website to absorb every single word; rather, they quickly glance over pages to see if you address their question or problem. So, use fewer words in each sentence (no more than 20) and fewer sentences in each paragraph. Also, use subheaders, bullet points, and bold text (sparingly) to make the content easy to scan.

While concise copy is the king of the readability castle, you shouldn't sacrifice the queen: *interesting* copy. To make your website text friendlier to prospective customers:

- Use different words at the beginning of consecutive sentences.
- Vary sentence length.
- Avoid passive voice.
- Use transition words.

Content Marketing

As you might recall from Chapter 3, content marketing basically flips old-school advertising upside down. Rather than pitching your services and waiting for customers to hand you a check before you offer them help, you come at it from the other direction. You offer valuable, meaningful content *for free* to build trust and credibility and to help people solve their own problems. I know, I know: It sounds crazy. But it *works* when it's done correctly.

Content marketing is a strategic marketing approach focused on creating and distributing valuable, relevant, and consistent content to attract and retain a clearly defined audience—and, ultimately, to drive profitable customer action.[6]

Content Marketing That Works

To make the most of content marketing:

- ☐ **Be consistent.** Publishing one blog post every three or four months (or whenever you feel like it and have the time to do it) is not an effective content marketing strategy.

  - ○ Develop a sustainable rhythm that works for you, and stick to it.

  - ○ Set yourself up for success by building a quarterly editorial calendar that lists at least one piece of content for each week. There's nothing worse than sitting in front of a blinking cursor, racking your brain for ideas.

  - ○ Try to work at least a week in advance so you can let your content sit for a couple of days before you review it, make changes, proofread, and publish it.

- ☐ **Vary the types of content you offer.** For most plumbing and HVAC shops, blogging is the default tactic. There's nothing wrong with posting written content, but it's good to switch it up from time to time.

  - ○ Rather than writing a step-by-step, DIY preventive maintenance post, could you do a quick video or SlideShare to show prospective customers what you're talking about?

  - ○ How about an infographic to illustrate a topic?

  - ○ Could you do a Facebook Live post to answer some plumbing or HVAC FAQs?

○ What customer success stories could you share?

☐ **Be helpful.** Brainstorm a list of questions customers have asked you in the past, and begin by answering those questions. Content marketing only works if you're publishing helpful, useful information, so think about your customers first.

☐ **Close the loop.** While content marketing is intentionally not sales-pitchy, you nevertheless need to help people move down the funnel and toward a conversion if/when they're ready to do so. So, link your pieces of content to one another and to calls to action.

Blogging

Blogging is an easy on-ramp to content marketing for most HVAC and plumbing shops. Just in case you're not convinced blogging is a necessary addition to your digital strategy, let's first cover-off on the "why" of blogging.

1. **Blogging helps you get found.** Once upon a time, if someone needed a contractor, they'd flip to the yellow pages, choose a company that sounded vaguely familiar, make a call, and keep their fingers crossed. These days, people open Google (usually), and they either type, "HVAC or plumbing companies in [their town]" or they ask a question like, "How do I clean my HVAC compressor or unclog my toilet?" Google will serve up your website in the search results if you've done a good job with SEO **and if you're consistently adding fresh content to your website.**

   That second "if"? That's where blogging comes in. Google doesn't love static websites. By adding new, quality content to your site on a regular basis, Google's algorithms see it as worthwhile and relevant. That means the search giant is more likely to show your site to your potential customers. That's a big deal.

2. **Blogging establishes you as a trustworthy expert.** By offering solutions to people's HVAC or plumbing problems via your blog, potential customers will experience you as a helpful company whom they can trust not to rip them off. How so? Well, if you were in the business only to make a buck, why would you tell people how to fix something themselves?

    I can guess your pushback here: "But I *do* have to make money. This is my business, after all. So, yeah—why am I giving away valuable advice for *free*?" That's a great question. The honest response is, "That's the way the world works." You can head to YouTube and find DIY videos for nearly everything these days. Since people are already looking for DIY advice, it's good for them to get that advice from *you*. That way, when they reach the point of needing help, you'll be the company they call.

3. **Blog content can be repurposed for social media.** Your blog posts can be sliced up into bite-sized pieces to share on your social channels—which is where your current and future customers live. By actively engaging on social media—with a customer-first approach—your customers and leads will see your content more often. And being seen is half the battle.

4. **Blogging tells your company's story.** If you're strategic with your blog posts, potential customers will get a feel for you as a company—your character, your expertise, your experience, how you treat your customers, whom you employ, and more. Business is relationship-driven, and blogging gives you an opportunity to begin developing that relationship before a lead ever picks up the phone to call you.

Convinced? Great. Now, for blogging to "work," you'll need to approach it purposefully. Here are some tips:

☐ **Be patient.** It's important to say this up front: While blogging can be an effective way to connect and reconnect with customers, that's not going to happen overnight. Building anything of value takes time, and blogs are no exception. It may take several months to see an uptick in business directly tied to your blog.

☐ **Post weekly.** First, let me remind you that Google's ears perk up when it sees frequent updates to a website, and when Google notices you, the search giant is more likely to show you off to potential customers. **Again, frequent, regular website updates via a blog are extremely helpful to SEO.**

So, what does "frequent, regular updates" actually mean? As with all things marketing, the answer to that question is in constant flux. Currently, experts recommend you blog at least weekly. That's great advice if that's a sustainable pace for you. If it's not, or if you're not sure you can maintain that schedule longterm, start with fewer posts each month.

And then there's the question of how long each post should be. Honestly, that also depends on whom you ask. In general, longer, keyword-optimized—not keyword-*stuffed*—posts tend to get more traction, as long as it's valuable content. In other words, 1000 words of gobbledygook won't get you anywhere. But neither will too-short of a post, regardless of how well it's written.

Optimal blog length also depends on the specific topic you're addressing and how many words your competitors are writing about it. As of today, a helpful strategy is to write more—better. That may not be the case for long, though; as Google refines its algorithms to account for increased mobile usage, it'll likely revert to prioritizing shorter posts.

☐ **Be customer-focused.** Put yourself in your customer's shoes and brainstorm topics you think they'll be most interested in. Chances are, they'll care more about how to choose the best furnace filters or bathroom faucets than they will about industry trends. Allocate some time every month to brainstorming relevant, timely post topics.

☐ **Write well.** The readability tips I mentioned earlier apply to blog posts, too. Be concise. Write in plain English. "Chunk" text so it's scannable.

☐ **Be inviting.** Finally, be sure to include a call to action in every post. Let customers know you're the expert in your community, and you're happy to help them solve their HVAC or plumbing concerns. Tell them exactly what you want them to do: schedule an appointment, request a free estimate, and so on.

Calls to Action (CTA)

None of your marketing matters—not one little bit—if people can't figure out how to contact you to take the next step. *Every single piece of marketing you do should come with a next step.* That doesn't have to be a hard sell like, "Call us today to get a quote." It could be a less in-your-face CTA like, "Learn more about drain issues from this blog post." The exact CTA depends on two things: where people are in the conversion funnel and what your goal is for the specific marketing piece you're working on. Effective CTAs share some common characteristics:

☐ **Immediate.** CTAs should allow someone to take immediate action—whatever that action might be. Don't make people click four times to send you an email, and don't bury your phone number only on a "Contact us" page.

☐ **Obvious.** If you want someone to click a button on your website, make the button obvious. Use a contrasting color, make it large enough it can't be ignored (within reason, of course), and be clear with the button text: "Schedule a service call."

☐ **Mobile-friendly.** Remember that at least half of your prospective customers are viewing your website on their phone. So, don't just type out your phone number; make it a clickable/touchable link by updating your HTML:

    ○ `<a href="tel:1-555-555-5555">1-555-555-5555</a>`

    ○ `<a href="tel:1-555-555-5555">Call now.</a>`

☐ **Enticing.** Without getting overly sales-pitchy, try to entice prospective customers into taking action. Start your CTA with a verb, and the word *free* helps: "Get your free estimate."

☐ **Human-centric.** When developing your CTAs, ask yourself why your customer should take action. What benefit will they receive? What's their motivation? In addition, speak directly to your prospective customer. In the example above, notice I wrote, "Get *your* free estimate" not "Get a free estimate."

On-Demand Customer Service

As I mentioned in Chapter 3, customers expect to have 24/7 access to the businesses they deal with. Generally speaking, many people expect to be able to meaningfully connect with a company via email, via Facebook, over the phone, and in person. For marketers, this is a bit of a double-edged sword: It's great to have so many ways to connect with customers in beneficial ways, but it's crazy stressful to figure out smart ways to do this without bloating up on manpower.

Massive companies like Target or Amazon have robust CRMs that enable to them to seamlessly interface across platforms, track engagement, measure customer loyalty, and maximize lifetime customer values at every point of contact. But most HVAC and plumbing contractors I talk with don't have the pocketbooks to support that sort of customer relationship process.

To meet that demand, many companies are beginning to incorporate chatbots into their customer service strategy—automatic messaging systems that imitate conversations with customers. While some home services industry influencers suggest contractors don't need to make the leap to full-blown chatbots, it's still worth considering how to make it easier for customers to access you. I recommend free chat options like Tawk.to.

Retargeting

As I've said before, the purpose of your website is to convert leads into customers. Obviously, the first step is getting them to your site to begin with. For service customers, if you've been purposeful with your site content, conversion will likely happen the first time they drop by. They have a problem—usually an urgent one—so they're anxious to get someone in to solve it.

It's different for install and commercial customers, though. They have *time*, remember? You may not be the first company they've researched, and chances are good you won't be the last. So in this case, it's important to keep reminding them that you exist and why they should like you.

In marketing-speak, that's called *retargeting*, and you've likely experienced it. Let's say you have a dog, and recently you've been browsing the internet for a cute little outfit he can wear for your annual family pictures. (I don't know how likely it is that you dress your dog, but stick with me.) You visit a pet store website in the morning and then, *it's so weird*, you see Facebook ads for dog sweaters that same afternoon. *Whoa.*

Yeah, that's retargeting and it begins with *cookies*—little bits of information websites deposit on your device when you browse the internet: how many and which pages you clicked on, how long you stuck around, if you logged in, and so on. The next time you visit that same website, it'll take a peek into your computer to see if you've been there before and, if so, what you did while you were there.

This isn't as malicious as it sounds. Cookies don't contain any of your personal data; they only contain your history with a particular website. Also, you can block cookies through your browser settings, and with new privacy regulations, you have to give explicit permission for a site to drop cookies on your hard drive.

Over time, a particular cookie, or collection of cookies, puts you into an audience—which advertisers can access to deliver particular, targeted messages they hope you'll find relevant. Again, this isn't as big-brother as it may seem. Your cookie "profile" is completely anonymous. Marketers don't know exactly whom they're targeting—in terms of your name, contact information, and credit card numbers. They only know your browsing behavior and some of your preferences (e.g., you appear to have a dog and be the type of person who clothes pets).

In the case of your "coincidental" Facebook ad experience, that pet store was using a similar tool called the Facebook Pixel. Their website left a little piece of code on your computer that alerted their Facebook Ad account that you'd been to the website and were looking at doggie sweaters. In an attempt to draw you back to the site to make a purchase, it served you a relevant ad.

In Google Ads, retargeting is officially called *remarketing*, and these highly purposeful, personalized ads can bring big success with install and commercial clients—if you're patient and set up your ads for optimum effect.

YOUR NEXT STEPS

Mobile Responsiveness

☐ If your site isn't mobile responsive, now is the time to do something about it. *You should fix this before investing resources anywhere else.* There's no sense spending PPC dollars to send people to a site that doesn't work.

☐ Check Google Analytics to see what percentage of your traffic is currently coming from desktop vs. mobile sites. (I see your deer-in-the-headlights face. I cover Google Analytics in Chapter 10.)

Readability

☐ Invest in a readability analysis tool such as Hemingway Editor or, if you have a WordPress site, the Yoast SEO plugin. These tools offer specific, immediate feedback to dramatically improve your copy.

☐ Read every page of your website aloud. As you encounter awkward or difficult-to-understand passages, revise them.

☐ See if you can find long paragraphs to break into pieces, and/or try bullet-pointing some sections.

Content Marketing

☐ Brainstorm 10 blog topics. Write up three of them for your blog. (Save the other ideas for potential backlinks—which you'll learn about in the next chapter.)

☐ If you're simply not a writer, explore options for outsourcing this part of your marketing strategy. It's worth paying someone to create consistent, compelling content for your website and social channels.

- ❐ Open Excel or Google Sheets and start an editorial calendar. Don't over-think this: As you come up with content ideas, start slotting them into a schedule. That way you'll never be without a starting place on blog day.

Calls to Action

- ❐ Review your CTAs. Are they as clear and obvious as you once thought?

- ❐ Look through other reputable websites and notice how they "call to action." Can you adapt their ideas for your own goals?

On-Demand Customer Service

- ❐ How easy is it for customers to reach you? Is there a way to make it even easier?

- ❐ What's your average response time when customers make an inquiry through your website or Facebook? What can you do to shorten that response time?

Retargeting

- ❐ Try a Facebook Pixel ad. Visit facebook.com/business and search "using facebook pixel" to get step-by-step instructions.

- ❐ Try setting up a retargeting campaign on Google Ads.

CHAPTER 6:
BOOSTING ORGANIC SEARCH

Although Google's not the only search engine on the field, it's carrying the ball nearly 75% of the game.[1] Since three out of four people who need plumbing or HVAC services are using Google to find them, it's worth focusing your SEM energy (and budget) here first—and primarily.

The goal of your SEM strategy is, of course, to land at or near the top of the SERP. Traditional SEO practices—which is what I'm focusing on in this chapter—will help improve your SERP position *eventually*.

Allow me to commiserate for a moment: *Eventually* can feel frustrating, and I know you want to start growing your customer base *right now*. I'll help you do that in the next chapter through things like PPC Google Ads campaigns. **But if you want sustained results from your digital marketing, you'll have to be a bit patient.**

So, let's cover some organic SEO tactics.

Google My Business/Maps

Google My Business (GMB) is an anomaly in our typical "you get what you pay for" world: **It's both free *and* useful.**

When people search "plumber near me" or "heater repair [your town]," Google will deliver a set of three results toward the top of the SERP called the "map pack" or "3-pack," and it looks like this:

Super eye-catching, isn't it? Why would anyone bother looking past these results? Right: Most people won't. To have a shot at being included in the 3-pack, you *must* be on GMB.

Of course, many companies are starting to catch on to the power of GMB, so the competition for those slots is increasing. Google pushes more "prominent" businesses to the top of the pack, and it makes that determination based on your overall search ranking and by what it can find out about you online through directories, links, reviews, and more. **All of the SEM tactics I'm covering in this chapter will improve your chance of being in the map pack.**

Google Reviews

Personal recommendations convert at a 1:1 ratio, and as far as prospective customers are concerned, online reviews count as personal recommendations. That makes the reviews part of your GMB profile massively important.

Keyword Analysis

Keywords is just marketing-speak for the words and phrases people search for. Keywords for plumbers include things like *leaking faucet, clogged drain, best water heater, plugged toilet,* and *emergency plumbing service.* For HVAC, think *furnace repair, duct cleaning, air conditioning, heat pump,* and so on.

You'll want to include keywords all over your site—on landing pages, in blog posts, in the back-end HTML—but only in meaningful ways. Making sure your website is (appropriately) keyword-rich makes it easier for search engines to match someone's question with your answer. To really do this well, each page should be focused on only one target keyword. For instance, "water heater repair" and "tankless water heaters" should each have its own page.

Pro tip: Make sure you include "plumber [name of your town]" or "HVAC [name of your town]" on your homepage and services pages. These are called "geo modifiers," and when someone types in that phrase, they're most likely ready to hire someone *right now.* So, it'd be good for your shop to show up in their search results.

Keyword Density

To Google, "meaningful" and "appropriate" use of keywords has to do with *density.* Once upon a time, marketers tried to trick search engines by stuffing websites with keywords—literally repeating keywords randomly in the middle of sentences in completely nonsensical ways. They didn't care that the copy didn't read well; all they cared about was that Google found their website and showed it to potential customers.

It wasn't long before Google waved its finger at marketers all "nuh-uh-uh"-like and made it clear that keywords aren't the end-all-be-all of SEO.

Good content is. Google wants to make sure it's serving consumers well by providing them with helpful information, not keyword-stuffed gibberish.

HTML Analysis

The easiest way to get prospective customers to your website is via Google. But first, Google has to know your website even exists, and a lot of that has to do with the HTML running in the background. While a full explanation of HTML is beyond the scope of this book (and not at all interesting to any HVAC and plumbing pros I know), it's important to have a general understanding of some key pieces Google cares about.

Basically, HTML tells your website what clothes to wear. It dictates things like the color, size, and arrangement of text; the size and placement of pictures; where new paragraphs should begin; and so on. Google doesn't care what the code is, but it definitely cares what the code *represents*.

As you know, Google wants to deliver *meaningful* results on SERPs. A lot of that has to do with your choice of keywords, as you now know. But it also has to do with the HTML code surrounding those keywords, also known as *keyword prominence.*

Headers and Keyword Prominence

HTML header tags look like this: <H1>, <H2>, <H3>, etc. The most important header on the site—which is typically the largest and most eye-catching—is tagged with <H1>. The next highest level is <H2>, then <H3>, and on through <H5>. In practice, it looks something like:

<h1>[Your City Name] Air Conditioning Repair</h1>
<h2>We're the Best!</h2>

Which, if your site's Cascading Style Sheets (CSS) is formatted correctly, should look something like this:

[Your City Name] Air Conditioning Repair
We're the Best!

Placing keywords inside header tags gives them *prominence*, something web developers have long assumed Google cared about. Whether that's *actually* true is debatable, but even if it's not, putting keywords in headers is a good SEO tactic for another reason. We know Google ranks sites based, in part, on how long people stay on them. The longer they stick around, it reasons, the more valuable your content must be. Well, because consumers are an impatient bunch, if a website's content is arranged in long paragraph after longer paragraph with nothing breaking up all those words, they'll likely hit the back button and try another site.

Google keeps an eye on those bounces, and too many of them will hurt your site's reputation. So, using headers breaks your web content into scannable bits, which allows potential customers to see quickly if you're the solution they're looking for—and helps them stick around if you are.

The no-keyword-stuffing rule applies here, too. Don't create headers just for the purpose of boosting keyword prominence. Ultimately, headers are for your readers, not for Google.

Metadata

Your website's metadata, which literally means "data about data," gives Google an at-a-glance description of your site's content. In the HTML code, metadata appears as tags, just like in headers. The most important ones to use and maintain are:

- ☐ **Title tag: <title>.** Your title tag tells Google what your site's about, and it's also the first thing people notice on SERPs. Titles need to be descriptive and helpful to both Google and to people who have a problem you can solve, but they must also be concise; currently, title tags are limited to 55 characters. If you can work a keyword in here, *naturally*, all the better.

- [ ] **Meta description: <meta name="description" content="[Your site description]"-/>.** On a SERP, your <title> shows at the top of your listing. Next comes your URL, followed by your meta description. This description should set you apart from the others above and below it, so write it carefully.

Taggart Plumbing: Your Favorite Pittsburgh Plumber - Same Day Service
https://taggartplumbing.com/ ▾
5-Star Reviewed Pittsburgh Plumbers. **Taggart Plumbing** can handle all your repair and installation needs. With 24/7 Emergency Service and Financing Options.
Contact Us · About Us · Services · Service Area

Admittedly, meta descriptions are a bit of a puzzle in SEO-land. At one time, web developers advised us to keep them to 150-160 characters because that's all Google would display on the SERP. However, late in 2017 things started to change: Google now *sometimes* displays as many as 350 characters, and it doesn't *always* pull from the description tag. Sometimes, it shows text from the first paragraph on the actual page instead. Oh, Google!

This is a perfect example of why you can't take a set-it-and-forget-it approach to your digital marketing—and to your website, specifically. I know it seems like you should just be able to hire someone to put together a site for you and then you're "done." But Google and its algorithms are fluid; if you aren't paying attention and making adjustments as necessary, your site will, for all intents and purposes, disappear.

By the way, many web marketers insist meta descriptions have no effect on SERP rankings. Even if that's true, they still play an important role in digital marketing. A well-written description, when displayed on the SERP, can positively influence click-through rates. If you want more prospective customers to land on your site, it's worth using this tag.

☐ **Robots <meta name="robot"'" content="index, follow" />.**
"Robots" refers to special files or instructions for browsing your website that are *purely intended for Google*. Your customers will never see your robots.txt, but they *will* notice the impact of Google having a solid understanding of what your website is about and what pages are most important. Generally speaking, you want your site to allow the search engine crawlers to *index* and *follow* its pages (see the code above). The only pages you do *not* want to index are the ones to which you're driving only paid or referral traffic.

Images

SEO isn't just about words; photos and videos matter, too. Optimizing the visual elements of your website gives you yet another shot at being found by prospective customers, and if your site's attractive, you may even see more conversions.

Here are the most important image-related concepts for you to know:

☐ **Images needs to be the right size.** While it's important to have high-quality images, going overboard on file size can massively slow down your site's load-time, which could ding your SERP rank. Image file size is determined by the file type, the physical dimensions of a photo, and the type of compression used.[2] Your website should also allow for responsive images so they load quickly on mobile devices.

☐ **Metadata matters here, too.** Using accurate and complete metadata for your site's visual elements is every bit as important as it is for text. The name of each image should be meaningful (not just IMG_1425.jpg) to help Google make sense of it. In addition, there's a group of image-related tags collectively called *alt attributes*. The content of these tags display when your images don't load or if someone's using accessibility software, and they're a great place to include (but not *stuff*) keywords:

- ☐ **Title text.** Typically, your title text is the same as the image name, but because it's for people, not Google, use spaces between words so it's easily understood.

- ☐ **Alt text.** An image's alt text describes what's in the photo. Try to make your alt text clear and descriptive. If you can use a keyword in that description (without it sounding forced), all the better.

- ☐ **GPS tag away.** Use software like Adobe Lightroom to embed GPS coordinates of your business in the photos you publish. This not only helps your local SEO results, but it also positively affects your map pack ranking.

By the way, removing *unnecessary* metadata from photos and videos, such as camera settings, can help accelerate your load times.[3]

- ☐ **Context is helpful.**[4] As far as Google's concerned, random photos aren't useful. But if a photo seems to match someone's query *and* there's content immediately surrounding that photo that *also* seems relevant to the search, it gets excited. We like to make Google happy. When Google's happy, it brings you more leads.

- ☐ **Stock photos are never the best idea.** While Google may not be able to tell if the images on your website are original, most of your site visitors probably can. As I mentioned earlier in this book, authenticity matters, and your potential customers want to know the *real* you—not the happy-smiley "you" they've seen on other companies' billboards and websites.

Structured Data

Google indexes billions of websites, and it greatly appreciates super-organized (structured) data it can process quickly. Structured data belongs in the header content of your website, and your site visitors won't see it (unless they're super nerdy and know how to view your HTML). If you're using JSON-LD, which Google recommends, it'll look something like this:

```
<script type='application/ld+json'>
{
  "@context": "http://www.schema.org",
  "@type": "Plumber",
  "name": "Joe's Plumbing Shop",
  "url": "www.fakeplumbingwebsite.com",
  "logo": "www.fakeplumbingwebsite.com/logo.jpg",
  "description": "Joe's Fake Plumbing Shop is the best fake plumbing shop in the entire area!",
  "address": {
    "@type": "PostalAddress",
    "streetAddress": "134 Canutakemeto",
    "addressLocality": "Funkytown",
    "addressRegion": "IA",
    "postalCode": "55555",
    "addressCountry": "USA"
  },
  "hasMap": "embed:GMB_url_here",
  "openingHours": "Mo, Tu, We, Th, Fr, Sa, Su -"
}
</script>
```

Using structured data makes it really, really, *really* easy for Google to know what your site's about.

Backlinks

When another website links back to your website, that's called a *backlink*. In search engine world, backlinks are a big, big deal. Why?

Because if other people are linking to your content, that signals to Google that you're a trusted source of information.

More specifically, Google uses an algorithm called PageRank that counts how many links point to a website and assesses the quality of each of those links. Having lots of quality links means a higher rank on the SERP. In fact, the number of quality domains linking to a page correlates with search rankings more than any other SEO factor.[5]

Here's a plain-language recap:

- Things like *structured data* and *metadata* help Google see your website: "Oh, hey! There's a website here!"

- Keywords help Google know what your site is about: "Okay, so this site is about water heaters and sewer lines."

- Next, Google asks, "But do these people actually *know* anything about water heaters and sewer lines? Let's see what other sites have to say about that."

- Then, Google puts its feelers out, looking for validation that your site is legit. If other sites link to yours, it tells Google you have some authority on the topic being searched. Backlinks are the strongest indication of authority, and authority is foundational to SEO.

Not all Backlinks are Created Equal

It's important to note that not all backlinks carry the same weight with Google. In fact, there are more than 40 factors that may impact the relative worth of backlinks. As with most Google-y things, it's complicated.

For example, as you might expect, links from larger, more well-known sites carry more weight than links from tiny, obscure sites. If you were a restaurant, Google would get much more excited about a link from Zagat than it would about a link from a food blogger with four followers.

Here's a more complex example: Some backlinks include HTML code that tells search engines the link doesn't "count." These are called *no follow links*, and they look like this: <a href="http://www.website.com/" rel="nofollow">Link Text</a>.

If you're a nice person (and I believe you are), you're probably thinking, "Well, that's just terrible! Why would someone link to my site but tell Google to ignore it?" Long story short, the nofollow tag exists to cut down on spam. See, once people figured out how important backlinks are to getting higher search rankings, they started dropping their links all over the place—even in places that had nothing to do with their site's content. Well, Google doesn't appreciate that: Spammy backlinks hurt both the linker and the linkee. So webmasters started implementing automatic nofollow tags for things like blog comments.

Note: No follow links aren't completely worthless. While they won't garner you a bunch of authority "points" with Google, they'll nevertheless get you some referral traffic.

There are plenty of other unhelpful—and even detrimental–backlink types.[6] There's simply no SEO equivalent of "all press is good press," so it's important to do a backlink analysis from time to time.

Earning Healthy Backlinks

First, let's talk about how *not* to get healthy backlinks: **Don't pay for them.** What a pleasant surprise, right? The best backlinks are free! In fact, sponsored links must include that nofollow tag I mentioned earlier; otherwise, Google sees them as "link schemes" trying to game PageRank, and that makes the search engine super cranky.

Instead of paying for links, here's how to *earn* them:

☐ **Be patient.** If you're just beginning to ramp up your SEO efforts, it's going to take some time to develop street cred on the internet. Rightsize your expectations so you'll stick with your backlink strategy. And, in the meantime, invest some marketing resources in more short-term efforts like Google Ads. (We'll talk more about this in the next chapter.)

- **Do competitive backlink research.** If there's another shop in your service area that keeps blowing you away on SERP, it's likely they have more and better backlinks than you do. You need to find out what those are so you can build a competitive plan.

- **Create great content.** No one's going to link to your website "just because." Rather, they'll link to your site if you have valuable, entertaining, and/or timely information to offer to people who visit their site. Great blog content is a good place to start, but you can also create infographics, videos, quizzes, and step-by-step guides.

- **Answer the question, "Who cares?"** When you have good content to offer, figure out who'll care about it and reach out to let them know it exists. For example, if you have a post comparing different brands of water heaters, reach out the manufacturer of your number-one choice and let them know you're talking them up.

- **Offer to do guest posts.** Build relationships with relevant companies and organizations in your community, and offer to write guests posts for their websites. Think about great partnerships with home remodeling or construction companies in your area or local trade or business groups.

There's no doubt that developing a link building campaign is hard work. But remember: Backlinks are critical to SEO. If you want to improve your organic SERP—if you want people to know your shop exists and grow your business—backlinks are an essential piece of your marketing strategy.

Security

Google shies away from sites that appear to come with privacy or security concerns. Since 2014, site security has been a SERP ranking factor, but recently the search giant took things a step further: Sites not using SSL are now actually labeled "not secure" on Google Chrome. (Given that Chrome is Americans' desktop browser of choice, and second choice on tablet and mobile, that's a big deal.[7]) Aside from affecting your SERP rank, if your website URL comes up HTTP, rather that HTTPS (for "secure"), your potential customers may feel wary of sticking around.

Of course migrating your HTTP site to HTTPs can be a complex and costly process. But you know what else is complex and costly? Trying to stay in front of potential customers without a decent SERP rank. That may sound harsh, but I want your business to do well, and from a digital marketing perspective, you need Google's help. To get it, you'll have to invest in making your website secure. If you're not processing payments on your website, a simple tool to use for getting SSL security with minimum hassle is *Let's Encrypt*. It's not military-grade-bullet-proof stuff, but it's better than nothing.

CASE STUDY

Wortman Central Air partnered with a local news station to raise interest and support for local educators. How has that helped this shop grow? Check out **dpmarketing. services/game-changer** to find out.

YOUR NEXT STEPS

Google My Business (GMB)

☐ If you don't already have a GMB account, create one. To get started, visit https://www.google.com/business/, select "Claim Now," and follow the prompts.

☐ If you have a GMB account but haven't updated it in the past 90 days, do a quick audit:

   ○ Are your business hours and contact information still accurate?

   ○ Does your profile include some high-quality, interesting photos?

   ○ Are you using GMB posts to provide current maintenance tips and promotions to your customers?

   ○ Is your GMB map listing embedded on at least one page on your website?

Google Reviews

☐ Have you set up your GMB account yet? You'll need one to get Google reviews.

   ○ Ask every customer you've served in the last 14-30 days to leave you a review.

   ○ Compose an email that reads something like, "Dear [name]: It was our pleasure to be of help on [date]. We hope you experienced five-star service from [technician's name]! When you have a moment, could you please share your experience via a Google review? That'll help more homeowners find us. Thanks!"

○ Make it quick and easy for people to offer a review by linking directly from that email to your Google review form.

❑ Add a link on your website to your Google review form.

❑ Respond to every Google review—even just star ratings and even (especially) negative ones. (See Chapter 9.)

❑ Make asking for a review part of your customer care plan. Rather than aiming for having "100 reviews by the end of the year," focus on having a "slow drip" goal of two or three new reviews per tech, per week.

Keyword Analysis

❑ Visit Google's Keyword Planner to determine what words are most beneficial for your HVAC or plumbing business. https://ads.google.com/home/tools/keyword-planner/ (You will need an active Google Ads account to use this powerful and free tool.)

❑ Copy the text from one of your website pages into your favorite word processing software. Get a total word count, and then search for each of your focus keywords. If you're using any keyword more frequently than once every 200 words or so, edit your copy to make it less keyword dense.

HTML Analysis

❑ Add description tags to your website. If you already have them, review and revise the tags on your top 10 most viewed pages.

❑ Beef up the first paragraphs of your 10 most viewed pages. Make sure they include keywords, and shoot for

350 characters. The first 150 characters should offer sufficient information on their own, though, in case Google goes back to short snippets on SERPs.

☐ Does your site have a Robots.txt file that's current with your current pages? Have you submitted your sitemap for indexing through Bing Webmaster and Google Search Console?

Images

☐ Update all of your file names to make them relevant (ex: [city]-water-heater-repair.jpg).

☐ Add metadata to your website images.

☐ Consider adding a website plugin to help automate image optimization. (Ironically, you'll need to make sure that plugin itself doesn't slow down your site.)

☐ If you're currently using only stock images, hire a professional photographer to bring some authenticity to your site. It's not nearly as expensive as you might think, and you may be able to barter services.

Structured Data

☐ Talk with your web developer about adding JSON-LD code to your website.

Backlinks

☐ Remember those 10 blog ideas you brainstormed at the end of Chapter 5? Choose three of them to pitch as guest posts.

☐ Partner with a digital marketing company who can help you with your competitive research.

❐ Google "backlink checker," choose one of the available services, and see what links are pointing to your site.

Security

❐ Talk with your web developer about SSL.

❐ If your site is already secure, make sure you've also updated your local citations: Google My Business, Yelp, Angie's List, and so on. If your site itself is now HTTPS but local directories are pointing to your old HTTP, that doesn't do much for consumer confidence.

❐ Create 301 redirects with your domain registrar to ensure that your HTTPS is always prioritized over your HTTP site.

CHAPTER 7:
BOOSTING PAID SEARCH

When it comes to SEM, it's not organic or paid; **it's both.** *Forever.* However, the primary purpose of paid advertising is to kick-start and support your organic strategy. Typically, HVAC and plumbing companies can slowly decrease paid options as they gain momentum in other ways. **Your digital marketing budget should always include some allocation for ads, though.** Exactly how much depends on your goals.

Google Ads and PPC

Fun fact: 40,000 searches are conducted on Google every second.[1] Here's another one: The internet is comprised of more than 1 billion websites.[2] And one more: Landing an organic (read: *free*) spot on the first page of Google search takes time and effort. While most businesses are willing to put in the work, the waiting is another story. It's tough to be patient while your SEO kicks in and your reviews generate results.

That's where PPC ads through Google Ads come in. Done correctly, Google Ads will zip your website to the top of the search rankings immediately— above the organic searches. And here's the best part: You only pay for the ads when people click on them. In short, Google Ads offer high potential ROI with very little risk.

Think Google Ads aren't a big deal? Check out this web search for "Seattle Plumbers."

Did you notice that? The first *six* companies shown to this customer are from *ads*. The first organic result from SEO isn't until the tenth listing on the page.

So, yes, Google Ads are a big deal. *When set up correctly*, they'll bring you more leads every single day.

Setting Up Google Ads

When putting together your Google Ads campaigns, you'll be presented with many choices, and you'll need to make good decisions. While the goal is to get more traffic to your website, you don't want just *any* traffic; you want *qualified leads* to click on your ad.

Since Google is constantly making changes to its Ads platform, I'm not going to do a step-by-step walk-through of how to set up your ads. Instead, here's a checklist of a few things to watch for:

Location

Make sure you're targeting a particular geographical location with your Google Ads (typically your service area or a chunk of it). You don't want Google showing your shop to people halfway across the country.

Budget

One of the happiest features of Google Ads is that you get to decide how much to invest in your marketing efforts. However, it can be tricky to determine exactly what that budget should be. Even though you're only paying for each click on your ad, the cost of those clicks varies widely depending on the keywords you've chosen, if your competitors are using those same keywords, and what *their* budget is.

You see, Google technically uses an *auction* to determine how much you pay for a given click versus your competitor. Google looks to see which of its advertisers are using the keywords used in someone's query. Then it looks to see who's willing to pay the most for each of those keywords and, surprise surprise, serves up the ad that'll make them (Google) the most money. For beginners, it's wise to select the option to "Maximize conversions" and let Google determine how much your keyword bids should be, based on the daily budget you've established.

So how much of an investment should you make? **For contractors just beginning their Google Ads efforts, I recommend setting your first**

73

month's budget somewhere between $1,500 and $2,000—or about $50-65 per day. This will offer you a sufficient baseline test of your keywords, and you'll generate enough traffic to be able to track conversions. As you experiment and learn more about what ads actually generate results, you can adjust your budget from there.

Ad Groups

Within each Google Ads campaign, you can have multiple ad groups. For plumbing and HVAC shops, I recommend creating one ad group for each of your major service categories. Take advantage of Google's Keyword Planner, keeping in mind that keywords are simply the words and phrases your potential customers type into Google as they try to find a solution to their problem.

Ads

Next, you'll create individual ads within each ad group. Yes, there are ads within ad groups within campaigns. That hierarchy becomes more and more important the more pervasively you advertise with Google.

And right now you might be thinking, "Why do I have to create so many ads? Can't I just go with one and call it good?" No, and here's why: People will be using different search terms, so you'll need different ads to appear based on the specific problem people are hoping to solve.

Are Google Ads Actually Worth It?

There's no question that Google Ads are a short-term solution to getting your HVAC or plumbing company some search love while you're waiting for your long-term solutions to kick in. And yes, they're worth the investment if you set them up correctly, track your conversions, and make adjustments along the way.

Google: The Next Level

I've hinted multiple times that Google changes frequently. Some changes are relatively small and don't have a major, immediate impact on how your site performs in search queries. Other updates, though, have a massive, potentially devastating effect—if you don't act on them. Two recent updates fall into this category: Google Guaranteed and advances in Artificial Intelligence (AI).

Google Local Services and Google Guaranteed

At the very top of many search results is the newest addition to Google's product lineup: **Google Local Services**. When a potential customer types into Google "plumbers [your town]" or "HVAC [your town]," they'll see this at the very top of the page:

See that badge: **Google Guaranteed?** In early 2018, Google began testing this new program, and it appears it's going to stick around. To consumers, that badge is significant: It means a service provider has been pre-screened as trustworthy. Google puts their money where their mouth is, too: If a customer books a service call through Local Services and isn't satisfied, Google will issue a refund (with some stipulations, of course). Incidentally, business owners have some guarantees, too: You'll only pay for *legitimate* leads.

Earning the Google Guaranteed badge, and therefore claiming a spot at the top of the results page, involves three steps:

1. Purchasing Local Services ads.

2. Completing a background check.

3. Verifying your license and insurance.

Keep in mind, Local Services is not the same thing as your Google Ads PPC budget. It's an entirely different product with an entirely different purpose. PPC is pay per **click**; Local Services is pay per **lead**. But, unlike sites like HomeAdvisor—where you either have to race to the bottom in price or race to be the first to close a deal—each customer is verified as a lead and then *assigned* to one company.

The Google Local Services app offers a way for businesses to connect directly with their leads, schedule appointments, manage their Local Services budget, and more. Just keep in mind, **this is all pay to play.** Your business won't even show up in the app unless you're paying to be listed there. And, as you might expect, there are ways to optimize your Local Services listing, too, including getting more five-star reviews and promptly responding to inquiries.

Google Local Services and Google Guaranteed are rolling out now, with 30 major cities participating by the end of 2018. Because it's still so new, I'm not sure what percent of searches will land with Google Local Service companies. Time will tell. One thing's for sure: It's not something to ignore.

Google and Artificial Intelligence (AI)

In late 2017, Google announced you can now use Google Assistant to find local home services. That's right—your potential customers literally don't have to lift a finger to get the help they need, not even to type out a search query. In fact, not only can Google Assistant help people find what they need, but it also can call the company *for them*. Here's how it works:

- You tell Google what you're looking for.

- Google gives you some information and then asks if you'd like it to make a call or bring up a list of results.

- If you'd prefer a list, Google will ask you a series of other questions about, for example, your specific need and your service address.

- At any point in your conversation (!) with Google, you can tell it to make the call for you.

Pretty cool for homeowners, right? But what does it mean for your business? According to Google, companies will be "prescreened by Google and companies like HomeAdvisor and Porch." More than ever, you'll need to follow Google's rules, create incredible reviews and ratings to stand out from your competition, and make sure you're smart about how you're getting leads online.

Exactly how this new feature will work isn't fully known just yet. However, two things are certain:

- Customers will begin seeing *fewer* choices, not more, when looking for a contractor.

- You can expect other AI-heavy services (e.g., Siri and Alexa) to follow suit.

If your company has mediocre reviews and is buried on page three (or more) on Google, AI likely means *even fewer* leads from the internet. If your company has awesome reviews and can be found on page one *as well as other sources,* you'll probably get more leads.

YOUR NEXT STEPS

Google Ads

❏ Take a look at your marketing budget. Are you allocating a decent amount for Google Ads (at least $50/day)?

❏ When was the last time you checked your Google Ads conversions? If it's been longer than four weeks, take a look and see how your ads are performing.

Google: The Next Level

❏ Do a quick search for your services in your community. Are you seeing Google Guaranteed ads? How many of your competitors are already listed with Local Services?

❏ Pay attention and adapt. Don't become complacent with how you're spending your ad budget. Stay in-the-know about major changes like AI and Google Guaranteed so you can make adjustments to stay (or get) visible to your potential customers.

CHAPTER 8:
SOCIAL MEDIA

Social media has become such a given in our culture that it's difficult to remember what life was like pre-Facebook. What did we do while we watched TV? Before Instagram, how did we avoid making small talk with people at the market? Did we actually, like, *talk* to our friends and family during meals?

Whether you think social media is the best thing ever or the absolute worst, one thing's for certain: It's here to stay. It'll continue to evolve over time, of course, and in 10 years it may look and function completely differently than it does today. But there's no doubt that people are going to stay connected with one another online, far into the future. They're also going to stay connected to brands and companies—like yours—so it'd be good for you to know how to leverage social media to your business advantage.

Before we get to strategy, let me mention two key thoughts to keep in mind along the way:

- **Doing social media *well* takes time, energy, and effort.** To be honest it takes very little effort to set up a Facebook Page or Instagram account, add a couple of photos, and post an occasional coupon. But from that very little effort, you'll enjoy very little return. Social media can be an incredibly powerful tool *if* you're willing to work at it.

- **Social media will probably not bring you (many) new, qualified leads.** Online social networks are not good environments for your BOFU digital marketing strategy. However, they're terrific places to *introduce new people* to your company and to *stay engaged with your current service customers*—the folks who've already gone through your conversion funnel and whom you hope will stick around in your sales pipeline. (It's much easier and far less expensive to keep current customers than to get new ones, remember?)

When it comes to install and commercial clients, social media channels provide a MOFU touchpoint. They've heard of you, and they've done some initial poking around on your website. When they turn to your social accounts, they're looking for validation of their initial impressions of you.

The Why of Social Media

If the purpose of social media is *not* to get quick, qualified leads, then why should you invest all that time and energy? So many reasons:

1. **Your customers are using social media**. The first reason your plumbing or HVAC shop needs to be on social is simple: That's where your potential and current customers are. In 2018, more than three-quarters of Americans have at least one social account,[1] and almost all of those folks are on multiple networks.[2] What's more, recent estimates indicate the average person will spend more than five years of their life using social media.[3] So, yes: Your customers are on social networks— ready-made platforms where you can engage with them at several points along the conversion funnel.

2. **Social media is a place to connect—human to human.** Human-centric marketing is about authenticity and empathy, and social channels are natural media for those interactions.

3. **You can learn about your customers, competitors, and community through social media.** Social networks are not one-way; they're inherently two-way channels designed for both talking *and* listening. The social networks I recommend to HVAC and plumbing shops come with robust demographic analytics to help you better target your communication. Through social networks, you can keep an eye on your competition to learn how they're engaging (or not) with potential customers. Finally, through

tools like Google alerts and hashtags, you can listen in on—and participate in—conversations relevant to the services you provide.

4. **Social networks can boost SERP rankings.** By posting the right types of content (which I'll get to in a bit), you can drive traffic from your social accounts to your website. The more organic traffic you get, the more impressed Google is by you—and the higher your SERP rank climbs. Plus, people are more likely to convert on your website than they are on social media. Your social channels will help guide them to the right place when they're ready to make a decision.

5. **Social media is a way to boost credibility.** Sharing helpful content is a way to show your potential customers that you're knowledgeable and trustworthy. Reviews also help to boost your credibility, particularly if they're positive.

6. **You can manage your reputation through social channels.** Ninety percent of people who read online reviews say their purchasing decisions are influenced by them.[4] If you think that's not a big deal, consider that 91% of people regularly or occasionally read online reviews.[5] What people are saying about you online (or if they're saying anything at all) and how you're responding to that feedback (or not) could make a considerable difference to your bottom line.

7. **Social media offers another—and expected—channel for customer care.** With the rise of social media has come the expectation of 24/7 customer service. As reported by Forbes, nearly half of social media users have sought customer care via social media,[6] and a study by the Harvard Business Review makes clear the importance of responding—quickly—to both happy and angry customers.[7]

8. **Social media helps you waste less money on advertising.** Social media advertising is a relatively inexpensive way to reach extremely specific groups of people with your message. Remember to right-

size your expectations, though; "reach" doesn't mean "convert." It can, however, mean moving people farther down the funnel *toward* conversion.

The How of Social Media

I recently read that for too long companies have been all about *collecting* customers, rather than *connecting* with them. I couldn't agree more. We simply post too much about ourselves, using communication channels as a bullhorn to try to shout people into being our customers. *That simply doesn't work anymore.*

If you're going to bother with having a social media presence for your plumbing or HVAC shop, you'll see more results by using the "rule of thirds": one-third of your posts should be helpful content, another third should be posts that humanize your company, and the last third (at most) can be sales-y things like coupons and specials.

Helpful Content

The different social networks require different strategies. For example, business owners often ask me how often they should post, and my answer is, "It depends." If we're talking about Facebook, my answer is once per day. If we're talking about Twitter, though, my answer is—take a deep breath, now—15 times per day.[8]

More important than frequency, though, is consistently offering quality content. If all you're posting is stuff about you and your company, potential customers won't be able to unfollow you fast enough. But if you're sharing helpful information, DIY tips, and other valuable content, people will take notice and remember you.

The good news is you don't have to create brand new, epic pieces of content for every one of tomorrow's 15 tweets. Instead, get creative with how you *repurpose* content that already exists:

- ☐ Break recent blog posts into sound bites and make graphics to accompany them. (Yes, I said, "Make graphics." I'll suggest some tools for that later on in this chapter.) *Re-release content; don't rewrite it.*

- ☐ Create a helpful list and share one item off that list at a time.

- ☐ Retweet and share other people's high-quality content. Anything that's relevant to your industry *from a customer's perspective*—is fair game. Think HGTV bathroom remodeling hacks or energy-saving tips from energystar.gov.

Keep in mind that your posts don't *always* have to be about plumbing or HVAC. Mix things up by sharing entertaining, helpful, or meaningful content. For example, check out your town's website or Facebook Page, and share posts about what's happening this weekend. Or, remember that cool job your company did at the zoo? Post photos of your time there. That will give a nod to your credibility and, well, stuff like that is just awesome to look at!

Humanizing Content

While our connection to one another seems to be becoming more and more virtual thanks to technology, *people still do business with people, not companies.* However, those people are more skeptical than ever before (also thanks to technology, perhaps), and I said at the start of this book, there's just no such thing as business on a handshake these days. Fortunately, social media offers you the perfect opportunity to show potential customers you're the good guys. Use your social channels to humanize your company:

- ☐ Post photos of your technicians, along with fun facts about them.

- ☐ Share videos from your bring-your-pet-to-work day or your company picnic.

- [ ] If your shop is sponsoring a community activity or if your team is participating in a charity event, post about that:

  Coupons, sales, and gimmicks no longer move the needle like social entrepreneurship does. [Companies] with a conscience not only attract better talent and woo discerning consumers, but they also wind up building communities and boosting the bottom line.[9]

Sales Pitches

There's nothing wrong with sharing specials and coupons, but limit those types of posts to no more than one-third of your overall social presence. When you *do* post about your services, be creative about it, so it doesn't always feel like a sales pitch:

- [ ] Post photos of your service trucks with a "We're here when you need us" caption.

- [ ] Share links to your review page so people can see what other people are saying about you, instead of what you say about you.

- [ ] Along with a coupon or incentive, include some photos or a video of similar work you recently performed.

In case you just wrote *"advertise our loyalty/referral programs"* in the margins of this section, I'd like to share my soap-box opinion about those. Here's the simplest way I can think to say it: *The best way to earn loyal customers and gain their trust enough to refer their friends and family to you is by being the absolute best HVAC or plumbing shop around.* Focus on the value you bring your customers, not on the price you charge—so, if you're good at what you do, you should not have to compete for cheap work by giving away services through loyalty and referral programs.

Here's another way to say it: Don't incentivize people into becoming customers. There are no shortcuts to building a sustainable, profitable business. So instead of coming up with gimmicks to post on Facebook, focus on building systems that support a higher goal of being *the shop* in your community.

What systems? Customer relationship management and collecting customer data, using technology to engage with people and to offer them value even before they're your paying customer, managing your online reputation, and so on. **In short, develop *systemic* approaches to loyalty and referrals, not programmatic ones.**

The What and When of Social Media

Currently, there are *hundreds* of active social networks worldwide—no exaggeration.[10] Fortunately, plumbing and HVAC shops really only need to engage in the four biggies: Facebook, YouTube, Instagram, and Twitter. Each of these environments has its own demographics and personality, and it's worth customizing your content to suit each one.

User Statistics

Facebook[11]

▸ 2.2 billion monthly active users.

▸ 66% of U.S. adults use Facebook.

▸ Most popular with those ages 25 to 34.

▸ Slightly more women than men use Facebook.[12]

YouTube[13]

▸ 1.5 billion users, second only to Facebook.

▸ Nearly 75% of American adults use YouTube.[14]

▸ Most popular among 18- to 24-year-olds, but 66% of Americans 65- to 75-year-olds use the network.[15]

▸ 72% of women and 75% of men use YouTube.[16]

Instagram[17]

▶ 1 billion users.

▶ 32% of online adults use Instagram.

▶ 59% of Instagram users are younger than 30. 33% are 30- to 49-year-olds.

▶ 38% of American women and 26% of American men use Instagram.[18]

Twitter[19]

▶ 330 million monthly active users.

▶ 24% of U.S. adults use Twitter.[20]

▶ Most popular among 25- to 34-year-olds.[21]

▶ 21% of American men and women use Twitter.

▶ Slightly more men than women use Twitter.[22]

How People Use the Network

Facebook

▶ 47% of Facebook users log in from mobile devices.

▶ People use Facebook to see photos from their friends and family and to share their opinions with a broad audience.[23]

▶ They aren't necessarily coming to Facebook to find someone to fix their furnace or heater, although people are starting to ask for recommendations (if their problem is minor enough to wait for responses).

YouTube

▶ More than half of all YouTube views come from mobile devices.

▶ 65% of YouTube viewers use the site to "help me fix something in my home or car."

Instagram

▶ Although you can view Instagram on a desktop, the network is designed as a mobile app.

▶ People follow their *passions* on Instagram.

▶ 75% of Instagrammers take action after seeing a company's post.

Twitter

▶ 80% of Twitter users access the network on a mobile device.

▶ 93% of people who follow small businesses on Twitter plan to purchase from them.

▶ Tweets with videos are six times more likely to be retweeted than those with photos—which are half as likely to be retweeted as tweets with GIFs.

Content Tips

For all four social platforms, remember that people are engaging with social networks from mobile devices. That means people coming to your website via your social channels will be expecting a mobile-friendly experience. In case I haven't said it before (but I'm sure I have): If your website isn't responsive, that needs to be at the tippy top of your digital marketing to-do list. Fix that now.

Facebook

▶ Be sure to have plenty of reviews on your page.

▶ When using Facebook ads, target for a specific audience to avoid wasting money.

▶ Posts with photos receive 39% more interaction, and interaction means exposure. Translation? Avoid posting text-only updates.[24]

YouTube

▶ Create educational content for YouTube.

▶ While your videos don't have to be cinema-quality, they do need to have steady visuals and clear audio.

▶ YouTube is a great place to add backlinks (back to your website) for an SEO boost.

Instagram

▶ Share your shop's "voice" and personality. Behind-the-scenes posts are great for this purpose.

▶ Use hashtags to reach a wider audience—beyond those who follow your shop.

▶ Your customers aren't passionate about plumbing and HVAC. But they're probably passionate about taking care of their homes, saving money, and so on. You'll have to think creatively to create worthwhile Instagram content!

▶ CTAs are particularly important for Instagram posts, given how many users take action on posts. Unfortunately, Instagram doesn't allow you put links directly into your captions. So, be sure your Instagram bio includes the best, general URL for people to click on. Better yet, consider investing in a linkinprofile.com account so you can send people to specific landing pages based on their posts of interest.

Twitter

▶ Useful for direct communication with customers and with industry professionals.

▶ Using hashtags will help you reach people who aren't yet following you.

▶ Link clicks get the most engagement (92% of all user interaction[25]), so include a linked CTA when possible.

- ▶ Use video as often as you can. That doesn't mean you have to create brand new content for Twitter. For example, you can slice a piece out of a YouTube video and post that to Twitter.

When and How Often to Post[26,27]

Facebook

- ▶ Post no more than once per day and no fewer than three times per week.

- ▶ Every other day, your post can be shared or curated content.

- ▶ Posts made between 10 am and 3 pm on weekdays tend to see the highest engagement.

YouTube

- ▶ With YouTube, quality and consistency are more important than frequency. Determine a realistic video production schedule—whether weekly or monthly—and stick to it.

- ▶ Be sure to have an introductory video on your YouTube page to give users an immediate impression of who you are and why they should care about your videos.

- ▶ Since most YouTube users watch videos in the evenings and on the weekends, post in the early afternoon on Thursday or Friday or early morning on Saturday or Sunday. That will give the network a chance to index your new video before users get active.[28]

Instagram

- ▶ Post once or twice per day.

- ▶ Only post *original* content on Instagram. Curated/shared posts aren't as interesting to this audience.

- ▶ Posts made over the lunch hour tend to see the highest engagement.[29]

Twitter

- ▶ Tweet 15 times per day.

- ▶ Approximately half of your tweets can be curated content or retweets.

- ▶ Weekday posts tend to get the most engagement.[30]

Tips, Tricks, and Tools for Social Media Success

As you've been reading through this chapter, I imagine you saying, out loud, things like, "You want me to post to Twitter *how many times*?!" and "I'm sure videos and photos do get more engagement. So am I supposed to hire a professional arts team now?!" and "I have *actual work* to get done for *actual customers*, so how in the world am I supposed to keep up with all this social media stuff?!"

I feel you. I do. It really is hard work. But also, it really is worth the effort. And, you'll be pleased to know, there are all sorts of tools out there to help you execute your social strategy. Following is a semi-random list of those tools.

Tools for Photos and Videos

As I've said all along here, people want to do business with *human* companies. Authenticity rules the marketing day. So don't worry about creating award-winning photo and video posts. Instead, *be real*.

But please don't be *terrible*. I'm not talking about blurry photos and videos filled with static and echoes. I'm just suggesting that good is better than perfect, and it's definitely better than nothing at all. Check out these tools to help you create engaging posts:

- [ ] **Canva.** Web- and app-based design program that allows you to add text to images. Although you can pay for some features and templates, it's easy to create great social graphics for free.

- [ ] **Ripl.** iPhone app that creates animated quote images (so it's a bit like Canva on steroids). Free and paid versions available.

- [ ] **Adobe Spark Video.** Web and iPhone program that allows you to create simple videos, complete with voice-overs. Free and paid versions available. I'm a huge fan of this tool.

Tools for Scheduling

I don't know anyone who has time to sit at their computer every day and write social media posts—not even full-time digital marketers do that. Instead of putting up posts one at a time in real time, it's more efficient to use scheduling software:

- [ ] **Hootsuite.** With software like Hootsuite, you can sit down at the beginning of the week and pre-schedule social posts to appear in the future. With Hootsuite's free plan, one user can manage up to three social accounts and schedule up to 30 posts at a time. (Paid versions allow more users, more accounts, and bulk scheduling.) *Note:* Facebook no longer allows third-party posts.

- [ ] **Other third-party schedulers.** Honestly, there are a gazillion options for social post scheduling: Buffer, Sprout Social, TweetDeck, and many, many more. It's worth taking the time to explore your options. Don't compare just features and price; also take a look at the various user interfaces. You want to choose a solution you can stand to look at and that's nice and intuitive to use—or you *won't* use it.

- [ ] **Facebook Scheduler.** You can schedule posts for the future right inside Facebook.

Notes About Scheduling Social Posts

- ☐ Although tools like Hootsuite allow you to schedule posts in the future, you still shouldn't take a set-it-and-forget-it approach to your social accounts. You'll need to check in on every account at least once per day to respond to questions, comments, and complaints. Also, pay attention to what's happening in the world. There's nothing worse than having a light-hearted comment post to your Twitter account 30 minutes after a national tragedy.

- ☐ At the time I'm writing this, no scheduling software will post directly to Instagram. You can create posts in advance and ask the software to remind you to push the button to post them, but it won't actually *do it* for you.

- ☐ Do *not* post the exact same content to all of your social networks. You don't have to change things dramatically, but each network has a slightly different purpose and vibe, and your posts should reflect that. For example, hashtags belong on Instagram and Twitter, but not on Facebook.

- ☐ It's fine to repurpose content, but avoid the temptation to use software that automatically reposts the same content you used before. Each time you post something, change it up a bit: use a different accompanying photo, rewrite the headline, choose a different caption.

Tools for Analytics

Each of the social platforms I recommend home service companies use comes with its own analytics or insights features. *Use them.* The data you get about your audience and how they're engaging (or not) with your social posts is invaluable—particularly when you start spending ad money in these networks.

Also, consider using a URL shortener like bit.ly that allows you to see click data. It'd be good to know which posts get people to click through to your website, right? The easiest way to learn that information is by having a link tracker doing the hard work for you.

Creating a Content Calendar

It's great to have tools to help create content, to help schedule it out, and to assess what is and what isn't working. But we still have the minor problem of what kind of content to post and how to keep track of what you're posting, where, and when. While there are fancier tools out there, I've found good, old-fashioned spreadsheets work just fine.

First, develop a general content calendar so you don't have to sit and watch your cursor blink while you're racking your brain for some creative inspiration. Having a general framework with "themes" will help you every time you sit down to schedule your posts.

SUNDAY	Inspirational quote
MONDAY	Link to new blog post
TUESDAY	DIY tip (related to blog post if possible)
WEDNESDAY	Community event
THURSDAY	Behind-the-scenes of your shop
FRIDAY	Family fun (suggestion for things to do this weekend)
SATURDAY	Highlight another local business

Then, have a *day-to-day* calendar showing specific posts that looks something like this. You can plug content into this as far into the future as you'd like. For example, if you run across a list of upcoming community events, make yourself a note to share each of those events as they come up. You'll be surprised by how quickly this calendar can fill up if you sit down and really focus on it.

WEEK	BLOG TOPIC	FACEBOOK	YOUTUBE	INSTAGRAM	TWITTER
AUGUST 5					

WEEK					
SUNDAY					
MONDAY					
TUESDAY					
WED					
THURSDAY					
FRIDAY					
SATURDAY					

Now, I realize this might make your head explode, but I'm telling you, having a purposeful social content strategy is much easier when everything lives in one spot. *Pro tip:* Create this using Google Sheets so it's easy to share with your marketing team, digital strategist, and so on.

Reviews and Reputation Management

If you've paid any attention to previous chapters, you should be saying, "Hey, Ryan! You forgot to talk about social media reviews and managing your reputation!" First, congratulations for reading so carefully. Second, I didn't forget: I made it a chapter all its own. Turn the page to get started.

NEXT STEPS

☐ Create your own content calendar and fill it in for the next two weeks.

☐ Ten days from today, block out three hours on your schedule to fill in your content calendar for the next two weeks.

☐ Take a look at Hootsuite, Loomly, HubSpot, Sprout Social, and Buffer. Make a decision on which of these social scheduling platforms to use.

CASE STUDY

Culpepper Home Services, a new shop that launched in January 2018, uses social media to help potential customers make smart decisions about how to hire the right plumbers, to schedule appointments, and more. Learn the results of his efforts and get ideas for upping your social media game at **dpmarketing.services/game-changer.**

CHAPTER 9:
REPUTATION MANAGEMENT

When it comes to growing your HVAC or plumbing business, you can spend a nauseating amount of money on advertising—only to discover that all you're doing is building *awareness* of your shop. What you actually need to do is grow *interest* in your shop.

In today's skeptical-of-everything culture, there's really only one marketing approach that's (nearly) guaranteed to help you do that: Be really good at what you do and get all of your customers talking about you. These days, the "talking about you" part needs to happen online, and it's important that you pay attention to what's being said. Marketers call that *reputation management*, and in this chapter you're going to learn everything you didn't know you needed to know about it.

As I've mentioned a time or two (or 12), your potential customers care far more about what *other people* say about you than what *you* say about you. What's more, people make decisions based on their *impressions* of a thing more than on the *reality* of that thing—and those impressions come from, you guessed it, *other people*. In fact, 90% of people say they're influenced by positive online reviews[1] when they make purchasing decisions.

Theoretically then, someone who thinks chocolate malts are gross (their reality) could be persuaded to try one if a bunch of people—*even people whom they've never met*—seem to think a particular soda fountain has "OMG the best.chocolate.malts.ever. #chocolatemaltsFTW" (others' impressions).

Anyone else want a chocolate malt now? You see my point then.

The Power of Loyalty

In case you're not yet convinced that online reviews play a major role in landing new customers, check out these statistics:

- Ninety-seven percent of customers find local businesses via the internet, and "review sites are at the epicenter of 'near me' searches."[2]

- Ninety-two percent of consumers read online reviews for local businesses.[3]

- Only 13% of people would consider trying a business with a one- or two-star rating, but 94% will try a business with a four-star rating.[4]

- Eighty-four percent of people trust online reviews as much as personal recommendations.[5]

Remember, these are all *random recommendations*—the opinions of people whom your potential customers don't even know. Personal recommendations convert at a one-to-one ratio. So is it advantageous to offer plumbing or HVAC services worth talking about? Most definitely.

In the service industry, a lot of folks talk about *customer loyalty*. Most of the time, *loyalty* brings to mind *repeat*: As in, "Loyal customers are repeat customers." From a digital marketing perspective, I want to challenge you to take the idea of *loyalty* one step further. Not only do loyal customers come back to your shop in the future, but also they *bring new customers with them*. In fact, they'll send people to your shop even if they, themselves, never need your services again.[6]

Loyal customers will personally recommend your services to people in their immediate circles of influence, and they'll also be happy to sing your praises online for complete strangers to read.

What's Already Being Said About You?

Before I give you some tips on getting people to talk about your shop online, let's first learn what's already being said about you.

Keep in mind that you can pay someone to do all of this work for you—a digital marketing service or a company that specializes in online reputation management. Depending on the size of your shop (and your marketing budget), it might make sense for you to outsource these tasks. If you're just starting out and/or you're curious *right this minute,* these tips will give you a good start.

For plumbing and HVAC companies, it's absolutely critical to keep an eye on a handful of places:

1. **Google My Business.** No surprise here, right? If you have a GMB account, your star rating will automatically display with your SERP listing for all the world to see. For example, check out the SERP for "plumbers Raleigh NC":

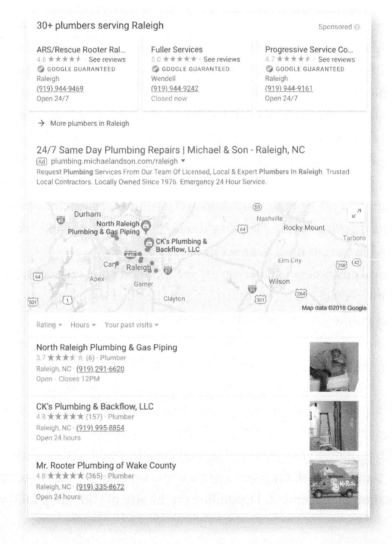

Notice that "See reviews" appears inside every Google Guaranteed listing, and when I click the first result in the map pack, I see a prominent link for "6 Google reviews":

North Raleigh Plumbing & Gas Piping

Website   Directions   Save

3.7 ★★★★ ⯨   6 Google reviews
Plumber in Raleigh, North Carolina

Address: 9021 Sweetbrook Ln Suite 303, Raleigh, NC 27615
Hours: Open · Closes 12PM ▾
Phone: (919) 291-6620

Suggest an edit

Know this place? Answer quick questions

Questions & answers
Be the first to ask a question   Ask a question

Google is the go-to review platform these days, with 64% of people indicating they're likely to read Google before visiting a business.[7] For this reason, **you should check for Google reviews–and respond to them—every day**. Yes, respond even to "just" star ratings. Why? Because star ratings are actually the number-one factor potential customers use to determine if they'll try a business.[8] And yes, you should respond even to—*especially to*—negative reviews. I'll teach you why and how later in this chapter.

2. **Google Alerts.** To be notified any time your shop is mentioned online, set up a Google Alert. Sometimes, this is the only way you'll know if someone's mentioned you/your shop in a blog post or has shared something you've written. Enter your name and the name of your shop at google.com/alerts, set how often and what time of day you'd like to receive alerts, and Google will email you whenever your shop is mentioned online. If your name or your shop's name is frequently misspelled, include alerts for those terms, too. *Pro tip:*

Set up alerts for your competitors to keep tabs on what's being said about them online.

3. **Social channels.** At least once per day, check your Facebook, YouTube, Instagram, and Twitter profiles for new followers, post likes and comments, and messages. All of these accounts allow you to configure push notifications to your mobile devices, and I strongly advise you to use them so you don't miss the opportunity to engage with current and potential customers. Respond to *all* interactions. *Fair warning*: If you manage to build a meaningful social presence, managing your accounts may feel overwhelming. Consider using a tool like Hootsuite so can you see all interactions in one spot.

4. **Yelp.** Yelp isn't just for foodies these days, so if you haven't claimed your business, do that today. It's free, easy, and it offers one more place you can show up in search results. Plus, the only way to respond to business reviews on Yelp is to be the business being reviewed.

5. **Blog post comments.** Set up your blog so it notifies you of new comments. If someone takes the time to engage with one of your posts, it's courteous (and potentially business-generating) to respond.

Getting Reviews

A 2017 global survey[9] showed that between one-quarter and one-half of respondents, depending on age, indicated they had posted an online review in the past month. Since it's gotten quicker and less complicated to post reviews, more people are offering them—and, you'll be happy to know, more people are taking the time to post *positive* ones.[10]

Asking for Reviews

That said, it takes four, five-star reviews to make up for every one, one-star review.[11] While I'm sure you offer outstanding customer service and unmatched value in your HVAC and plumbing work, it's possible that, at some point, someone's going to be having a bad day and will take it out on you.

Even if you don't end up with negative reviews, studies show more than 75% of consumers say reviews posted more than three months ago are irrelevant.[12] So, it behooves you to be proactive in your review-getting. What's that mean? *Simply ask for them.*

The most effective way to get someone to review you online is to **ask them in person** immediately following a service call with a happy ending. If your customer thanks you and says something particularly positive, respond like this:

That means so much to us. That kind of feedback helps our prospective customers feel more comfortable giving us a try. If you have a moment this week, would you mind sharing your experience on Facebook or Google?

Initially, your technicians may feel uncomfortable making such a bold ask, so you'll need to coach them a bit. Then, build into your sales routine a personalized, follow-up letter or email:

Dear [Name]:

Thanks again for trusting us to take care of your plumbing/HVAC needs. We feel lucky to have you as a customer, and we hope you're pleased with how we treated you and your home/business.

*These days, most people look for online reviews before they'll hire local companies, and **we'd greatly appreciate it if you'd take a moment***

to leave a star rating and a couple of sentences on Google, Facebook, and/or Yelp. *(If you can't give us four stars, that's OK, but please let us know where we missed the mark so we can make things right.)*

Thanks so much! - [Technician's Name and Contact Information]

In that message, make it as easy as possible for someone to leave a review by providing directions and, if you're sending the request via email, by linking directly to each of the review sites you mention. I recommend asking your customers to review you on:

1. Facebook.

2. Google.

3. Yelp.

4. Better Business Bureau (BBB). Although BBB doesn't get talked about much in digital marketing circles, it's a huge deal for contractors. You don't have to have an account with BBB to be listed with them, and having a connection with BBB adds SEO value to your website. (Remember all that talk in Chapter 6 about backlinks? The BBB is a great one to have.)

Paying for Reviews

Asking for reviews is one thing. *Paying* for them is quite another. My advice is to *not* incentivize (e.g., bribe) your customers into giving reviews—particularly positive ones. Facts are your friends, and if someone's had a less than stellar experience with your company, it's better for you to know the truth than to pay someone $10 to lie to you.

That said, there are a couple of service industry review sites worth including in your marketing budget if you can:

1. **Angie's List.** You can claim your Angie's List profile for free, and you can respond to reviews without a paid account. That's all well

and good, but chances are good no one will see you in Angie's List unless you pay for ads. Also, keep in mind that the number of reviews you've received doesn't show up unless you're a paid advertiser,[13] so even if people do happen upon your listing, they're unlikely to click for more information.

2. **Google Local Services/Guaranteed.** As I mentioned back in Chapter 7, Google Local Services is another advertising option with Google (separate from your Google Ads PPC campaigns). Being a Guaranteed contractor has significant reputation management perks, because that badge shows up on your GMB profile.

Obviously, there are plenty more directory options (HomeAdvisor and the like), but they're hardly worth mentioning compared to Google Local Services. There's no question you'll get the most bang for your buck by going with Google. Every time.

Responding to Reviews

Where reputation management is concerned, the key word is most definitely *management*. Asking for (or paying for) reviews is only the first step. To make reviews "work" to bring you more business, you'll need to engage with them—every one of them, every time. I can see that big question mark over your head about "every one, every time" so let's go ahead and start with the most counterintuitive situation.

Responding to Negative Reviews

On ReviewTrackers' recent customer survey, 94% of people indicated that a negative review has convinced them to stay away from a business.[14] Yikes, right? Fortunately, for most people a negative review only *stays* negative if you ignore it. Since you're likely thinking "Oh, yeah? Prove it," I'll toss you some data:

- One in three people name "responds to reviews" as a key factor when deciding to engage with a business.[15]

- More than half of customers expect businesses to respond to negative online comments within one week.[16]

- Up to 70% of people say they would give a company a second try if they saw them respond to a complaint, and that number jumps to 96% if the business offers a satisfactory resolution.[17]

And here's an interesting twist: Politely worded negative reviews actually *increase* the likelihood of someone giving your company a try. Weird, huh? But according to research, it's true: Reviews that begin with phrases like "I don't want to be mean, but…" are *helpful* to your business, not hurtful. And angry customers are more likely to give you *gentle* negative feedback if they see that you've responded kindly to negative comments in the past.[18]

You may be tempted to get defensive and even downright rude when you respond to negative reviews. Don't do that. Remember that while the customer may not always be right, the customer is always the customer. Treat them well—regardless of what ridiculous things they post on Google—and that review may actually grow your business.

Try these tips when you see not-great reviews:

- ☐ **Remember how many people are going to see your response.** Your responses to reviews are public, which means lots of people are going to see how you handle tough situations. If you lose your cool, the original commenter isn't the only one who'll know it.

- ☐ **Respond quickly.** Since you're checking your review sites daily (you are, aren't you?) you'll know right away if someone has less-than-flattering feedback for you. Respond to it within 24 hours or, if you need to cool off, within 48 hours. But don't wait longer than that.

- **Identify yourself.** It's easy for people to be angry with Hometown HVAC. It's more difficult for someone to stay angry with "Matt, owner of Hometown HVAC for 12 years."

- **Apologize.** Even if you completely disagree with someone's criticism, it's important to acknowledge their perspective and apologize. Keep it simple and sincere: "We are so sorry our technician was late."

- **Don't overlook star reviews with no comments.** If someone leaves a one-star review with no details, try a simple, "Oh no! It looks like we may have really goofed up. Can you let us know what happened?" If someone leaves a three-star review, respond like this: "Thanks for your kind rating. Can you tell us how we might have earned four stars from you instead?" More often than not, people will revise their review and give you that last star simply because you took the time to respond.

- **Offer an offline conversation.** When people are upset, a text-based conversation rarely results in a complete solution. Be sure to invite folks to call you so you can learn more about what happened.

- **Don't play point-counterpoint.** If someone posts a bullet-point tirade, don't address every concern. Instead, apologize and summarize. "Ugh. I'm so sorry to hear about your disappointing service call. What you're describing is definitely not our typical level of customer service. How can we make it up to you?"

Responding to Positive Reviews

When a customer's standing in front of you and they say something nice about their experience with your company, you respond, right? Why would you treat online reviews any differently?

- [ ] **Say thank you.** I don't mean to sound like your mother here, but use your manners. If someone offers you a compliment, the first thing out of your mouth (or off your keyboard) ought to be, "Thanks!"

- [ ] **Be specific.** Reviewers want to know they're hearing from an actual human being at the company, not a robot. So respond as specifically as you can. "Thanks for your kind words about Joe. He really does have a great sense of humor, and he genuinely cares about our Portland Plumbing customers."

- [ ] **Use keywords if you can.** Google crawls reviews, too, so while you shouldn't be ridiculous about it, it's good to work in a keyword if you can. "It's so great to hear how pleased you are with your water heater installation, Kim!" If you can naturally work in the name of your business, all the better.

- [ ] **Include a CTA.** Again, don't go overboard here, but don't be afraid to include something like, "Call us when you're ready to set up a preventive maintenance plan for that new furnace!"

Removing Reviews

In the vast majority of cases, it's better to respond to negative reviews than to try to get rid of them. However, if you encounter someone who, despite your best efforts, crosses the line of civility and/or is posting completely bogus reviews, try these steps:

- [ ] **Go offline.** If you're able to reach out to the person privately, send them a message asking them if there's anything you can do to improve their experience. If you're able to resolve the conflict, ask them to change their review. If there's not much hope for a fix, ask them to remove or revise any offensive comments.

- [ ] **Report the review.** Take a look at the terms of service for the platform where the review exists. If it's in violation of policies, report it or flag it as inappropriate. Be sure to keep an eye on the review every few days to see if there's any activity on it.

- [ ] **Get more positive reviews.** If you haven't asked recent customers for reviews, now is a great time to do so. On most sites, reviews are posted in reverse chronological order, so a flurry of positive reviews will nicely hide the ugly one.

- [ ] **Post a response.** If the reviewer won't cooperate and the website won't remove the comment, carefully craft a public response. "[Name]: We're bummed that we weren't able to reach a solution to this situation. We certainly hope you'll give us an opportunity to serve you better in the future." Your potential customers will be impressed to see you handle a difficult review with compassion and professionalism.

Your Street Cred

The reality is no one believes much of what they read online these days—other than reviews. You can talk all you want on your website about how great your service is and how much value you bring to your customers, but if you're the only one saying it, all that horn-tooting is unlikely to bring you a single new customer.

So the goal here is to make asking for reviews (and managing them) part of your *automated process*. This isn't a "sometimes do, sometimes forget" deal. This is an every-day-of-the-week, doesn't-matter-who-the-tech-is sort of thing. Your street cred is what matters to people. Manage it well.

YOUR NEXT STEPS

❒ Go check all of your accounts for reviews—GMB, Facebook, Yelp, BBB, and so on. If you have reviews to which you've not yet responded, set aside time this week to do so.

❒ Set up some Google Alerts to help you know what's already being said about you, your company, and your competitors.

❒ Create some templates you and your team can use to request reviews and respond to them.

CASE STUDY

Brian Wooten launched as a one-man shop with only a one-page website. While we worked on fixing that problem, we began an intentional effort to get him more Google reviews. After just 18 months, we had to go bigger-better with his website to support all the internet traffic he was getting. Learn more about his strategy and results at **dpmarketing.services/game-changer**.

CHAPTER 10:
ASSESSMENT

You and I have probably never met, but I bet I know something about you: You'd rather not spend a dime more on advertising than you absolutely have to. Me either. But as you've learned by this point, there are a number of ways to waste marketing dollars—many of which fall into one category: **Not Paying Attention.**

Maybe you paid someone to build you a really nice website a few years ago, but you haven't updated the content since launch day. Maybe you set up your GMB profile at some point, but you haven't actually gone back to check for and respond to reviews. Maybe you got some Google Ads going, but you haven't done any recent keyword research. I mean, when was the last time you Googled your shop? Do you have any idea where you're landing on the SERP these days?

The truth is, too many plumbing and HVAC shops take a set-it-and-forget it approach to their digital marketing. They get super excited about websites and social and SEO and all sorts of things, they get everything going, they invest a bunch of money toward all of it, they set the plates spinning, and then they never, *ever* think about any of it again. Meanwhile, plate after plate comes crashing to the floor—but sends you a hefty bill anyway.

Here's the deal: **Just because something *used* to work doesn't mean it's *still* working, and just because it's working *right now* doesn't mean it's going to work *next month*.** If you implement every strategy and tactic I've suggested in this book, I'd be willing to bet my last $20 and my first-born child that you'll see some positive results pretty quickly. But I'd also be willing to bet that if you don't *constantly* implement-assess-revise-repeat your plan, you'll see diminishing returns sooner than later.

The digital marketing space is inherently flexible. Algorithms change frequently. New technologies are introduced constantly. As prospective customers get more savvy, their behavior changes. Your competitors will look at what you're doing, and they'll try to copy you.

So, unless you have a bottomless pit for a marketing budget, you'll have to pay attention and be nimble to get the business-growing results you're looking for.

Facts Are Your Friends: Building an Assessment Plan

A marketing plan is only as good as its accompanying assessment plan. To avoid wasting money, you need to know what you're doing, understand *why* you're doing it, decide what you *hope to achieve* by it, figure out how to *measure* your progress, and then determine if you're getting any desired *results*. Those last three bits are the basic building blocks of an assessment plan, so let's break those down a bit.

Step 1: Set Your Goals

There's no doubt that the **overall goal** of a marketing strategy is to grow your business. But that's far too broad, so we need to be more particular. You may be familiar with SMART goals, but let's explore what they look like for HVAC and plumbing contractors.

SMART goals share five characteristics:

- ☐ **Specific.** What does "grow your business" look like? Are you okay earning 10 new customers this year? Or is that your monthly goal? Or weekly? Do you want to keep your eye on repeat customers, too? It's great to earn 50 new customers—unless you lose 45 old ones. Do you want to be busy enough to offer 24/7 service? Do you want to employ six more techs?

- ☐ **Measurable.** How will you know when you've reached your goal? Is there a revenue amount attached to "grow your business"? Number of service calls? Total number of customers? Number of referrals?

- ☐ **Attainable.** A good marketing strategy will point to an attainable goal. That doesn't mean it has to be *easy* to attain; but it must be *possible.* Be sure to consider the costs of achieving your goal as you're assessing how attainable it is. It might be possible to double your new customer base next quarter through Google Ads, but it's going to cost thousands and thousands of dollars to reach that goal. Is that really attainable?

☐ **Relevant.** This one's a bit more philosophical. A good goal should be relevant or meaningful *to you.* Why do you want to grow your business? Just because that's what good businesses do? Or because you want to retire early? Or because you want to give your technicians a bonus?

☐ **Timely.** A healthy goal will have a deadline. After you figure out the specifics, determine how long you want to give yourself to achieve them. Increase service calls by 20% in the next quarter? In the next year? It's fine to be optimistic when setting your timeline, but don't be totally unrealistic.

Step 2: Decide What Metrics to Use

Metrics is just a fancy word for *numbers.* I suggested a few up there, but there are some digital marketing-specific ones you should consider tracking, too. *Note:* It's easy to get lost in data points, so I'm focusing only on **Key Performance Indicators (KPI).**

Website-Related KPI

If you set a goal to, for example, increase traffic to your website (admirable goal) or improve your conversion rate from your website (even better goal!), Google Analytics (GA) will be your very best friend in the assessment process.

Helpful GA statistics include:

- [ ] **Total site visits.** How many "hits" your site received (in a time period you get to define) and how many individuals those hits represent.

- [ ] **Acquisition channels.** This section of GA tells you where your web traffic is coming from. It can both inform what outreach efforts you should consider and tell you if your current efforts are working.

- [ ] **Bounce rate.** Your bounce rate is a measurement of how many people stop by your site, check out whatever page they landed on, and then leave without taking additional action. This helps you determine if your web content is meaningful enough to customers–which will directly impact how much Google likes or dislikes your site.

- [ ] **Conversions.** Link your Google Ads and your GA accounts to learn if your ads are performing as well as you'd hoped and, if not, to get insight on how to fix that problem.

- [ ] **Top Landing Pages.** If you have any content-related goals for your website, knowing your top landing pages (the pages through which people enter your site) can help you decide where to focus your energy.

- [ ] **Dwell Time.** This is how long your web traffic spends on your site. The higher your dwell time, the better your SERP is likely to be. The better you provide great content for your visitors, the higher your dwell time will likely be.

- [ ] **Leads Generated.** With GA, you can actually create customer goals to help you know when you've created a lead. When a customer fills out a service request form on your site, for example, or when someone clicks from a smartphone to call your shop.

PPC-Related KPI

- ☐ **Clicks.** Duh, right? But really: You can't get a PPC conversion without first getting a click. So measure those. Also, try what's called A/B testing: Create two ads with slightly different wording, and see which one brings more clicks—then bump up your budget on the more successful one.

- ☐ **Click-through rate (CTR).** CTR is how many clicks you get as a percentage of impressions. If your ad is shown 10,000 times and you get only 5 clicks, that's not so great. But if you get 5 clicks after only 1,000 impressions, that's better. For context, anywhere from 1% to 2% is pretty decent. Get closer to (or above) 3%, and you're rockin'.

- ☐ **Quality Score (QS).** Arguably, this is the single most important metric you can track with PPC. The higher this number, the lower your cost per click will be.

- ☐ **Conversions.** If you're smart, you'll be using GA and Google Tag Manager to track your Google Ads traffic on your site. Knowing the conversion on your ad clicks is huge.

SEO-Related KPI

- ☐ **Keyword Rank.** Keyword rank is a measure of how well your site is performing in regard to your use of a particular keyword. The higher your keyword rank, the higher your SERP position when someone uses that keyword in their search query.

- ☐ **Domain Authority (DA).** DA is an indication of how well your site will perform in search, i.e., where you'll land on the SERP. If your SEO efforts are working, your DA will improve over time.

- ☐ **Page Authority (PA).** Like DA, PA predicts how well a specific page on your site will rank on SERP.

- [ ] **Total links built.** Backlinks are hugely important to your SEO strategy, as I discussed in Chapter 6. This KPI tells you if you're gaining any traction earning more links.

There are tons of tools on the web to help you determine and act on your SEO KPI. It's hard to go wrong with Moz (www.moz.com).

Social Media-Related KPI

When it comes to measuring the effectiveness of your social media strategy, you'll want to keep a close eye on the following data points:

- [ ] **Reach.** If one of your marketing goals is to get your company in front of more people on social media, *reach* or *impressions* will give you a fair estimate of the number of people who've seen each of your posts.

    Please note that word *estimate.* A billboard ad guy will promise you 40,000 impressions per day, but that's an estimate of how many people *drive by*, not how many people actually *look* at your ad. To put it bluntly, *reach* doesn't correlate with *profitability*, and getting 40,000 impressions isn't going to add even $1 to your bottom line.

    Nevertheless, measuring impressions makes sense if you're interested in understanding your overall visibility; after all, a potential reach of 40,000 is way better than a potential reach of four.

- [ ] **Engagement (likes, shares, and comments).** It doesn't matter if you have four kerpillion followers on every one of your social accounts if no one is engaging with your content. Likes, shares, and comments are an indicator of how much your message is resonating with your audience.

The Critical KPI Most Contractors Miss

When it comes to marketing strategy ROI, the only metric that *really* matters is how much it costs to gain a new customer. Hold that thought. I'll come back to it in a couple of pages.

Step 3: Assess Progress Toward Your Goals

Once you've established your goals and you've assigned metrics so you can tell if/when you've reached them, you'll need to track your progress periodically. In other words, you'll need to *look at your metrics, for crying out loud.*

I recommend looking at your data at least once per month. Set up some simple spreadsheets in which you can enter your data, which will allow you track your progress over time. It's really fun to see a line graph heading up and to the right. But remember that facts are your friends. If you're seeing a particular ad campaign tank, for example, you'll know you need to do something about it. Which brings us to the next step.

Step 4: Adjust Your Tactics to Improve Progress Toward Goals

Do not—I repeat, do *not*—adjust your goals prematurely. Since you're using SMART goals, you've established a time reference for each of them. If your progress toward a particular goal is slower than you'd hoped, the right move is to *adjust your tactic,* not your goal. If you had a goal to gain 10% more website traffic in six months, but by month four you're only seeing 6% growth, don't decide 6% is good enough; instead, try some A/B testing on your ad copy and adjust your campaigns from there.

Step 5: Assess Progress Again

Hey, guess what? After you make adjustments to your strategy, you'll need to check on how those new tactics are performing. Repeat Steps 3 and 4 for the entire duration you set for each SMART goal.

Step 6: Repeat

A month before your SMART goals expire, start drafting new goals for the next term—whatever that term is for you: the next fiscal or calendar year, quarter, month, or, if you're super fancy, fortnight.

The Truth About Return on Investment (ROI)

If the internet is to be believed (rarely), marketing ROI is relatively simple to measure. Well, I'm not going to lie to you: It's *not*. I mentioned in a previous chapter that this is a mix of science and art—but mostly science. I'm not backing up on that claim; building an effective digital marketing strategy should be a data-driven endeavor. However, it's not *all* science, and the art part makes measuring ROI a little interesting.

It helps to think about what ROI really means. It doesn't just tell you if you're getting enough bang for your buck. It actually helps you answer a bigger question: **Is the money you're spending generating the return you need** *at the cost you need it to happen*?

That's really helpful information, right? Once again: Facts are your friends. And some facts are more useful than others. Fortunately, there's one very clear metric that offers a sufficiently thorough picture of your digital marketing strategy's ROI.

Customer Acquisition Cost (CAC)

CAC or Cost of Acquisition (COA) as it's known in some circles, is **what it costs you to get one new customer**. This is a big-deal metric that a lot of companies avoid—out of ignorance or denial.

To discover your COA:

total all marketing expenses for the past 12 months
(billboards, websites, HomeAdvisor, everything)

then divide that number by:

**the total number of new customers you gained
over that same 12-month period**

Or,

Total Dollars Spent/Total Customers Gained

Poof. An *easy* metric that offers *critical* information.

Example: If you put all your marketing eggs in the billboard basket, spent $6000, and got only six new customers, your CAC is $1000. That's $1000 per customer. That's not a problem, I suppose, unless your average work order is only $450. (See why I say this is a big-deal metric?)

Keep in mind that CAC can skew a bit depending on the specific marketing tactics you're using. If you've just hired someone to help with SEO, that's a cost to include in your CAC—but you may not see results for several months after your initial investment. PPC ads, on the other hand, are more of a short-term strategy from which you'll get quicker (but more expensive) results.

Improving CAC

Bringing your CAC down isn't rocket science: minimize your marketing costs and maximize your earnings. The number-one way to minimize your marketing costs is to—say it with me—*pay attention*. Set goals, decide on metrics, assess your progress, make adjustments, repeat.

More specifically:

- ☐ **Improve conversion rates.** If only three customers convert on a campaign that ultimately cost you $3,000, that stinks. Bring your CAC down by adjusting that $3,000 campaign in ways that will bring you 30 more customers instead.

- ☐ **Increase referrals.** If Judy hires you for a job because her Aunt Sally referred her, your CAC for Judy is *half* your CAC for Sally. That's some good math right there.

- ☐ **Do more of what works.** If 70% of your web traffic is coming from a particular Google Ad, take bid dollars away from an under-performing ad (that's not generating any leads anyway) and put it toward the one that's working.

- ☐ **Go guerilla.** Not every marketing tactic requires money. Write more blog posts. Build more relationships in your community. Repurpose something you've already invested money in for a second, third, and fourth purpose. Every dollar you save improves CAC.

Qualitative ROI

I've written a lot about data in this chapter—a number of quantitative ways to figure out if your marketing plan is actually working. I can't close without mentioning an important—and ridiculously easy-to-use—*qualitative* tool.

You ready? Ask your customers one question: "How did you hear about us?" Track it. **Every time.** GA conversion stats can be complicated to sort through. A customer telling you they saw you on Facebook? Easy peasy.

YOUR NEXT STEPS

❒ Brainstorm some SMART goals for your digital marketing efforts.

❒ Start your KPI spreadsheet. If you're feeling overwhelmed by data, pick two or three metrics from each category (website, PPC, SEO, social media) and add a new one every quarter or so.

CHAPTER 11:
THE FUTURE OF DIGITAL MARKETING

Whew. You made it to the last section of the book. I imagine you feel like you've been drinking from a firehose since about midway through Chapter 1. It's a lot to take in, and you should definitely go get a beer. Or a root beer float. Or maybe just a nap.

Before I give you my best guess on the future of digital marketing, let me just give you a quick recap of where we've been.

Big Ideas

If you're feeling information overload, focus on the big ideas from each chapter.

☐ **Chapter 1: A Brief History of Digital Marketing.** The internet has taken away power from advertisers and given it back to your customers. They're now active participants, controlling their own flow of messaging.

☐ **Chapter 2: Your Target Customer.** People's decisions are motivated by only two things: money and emotions. Let that knowledge inform your human-centric, empathic marketing strategy.

☐ **Chapter 3: Your Digital Marketing Plan.** Your marketing plan needs to be diversified (omni-channel) to effectively meet customers at the different phases of the conversion funnel: awareness, interest, preference, conversion, advocacy. In other words, effective digital marketing plans are purposeful, matching a customer's place in the funnel to tactics that are most meaningful to them in that place. The goal of your digital marketing is to inspire folks to keep moving down the funnel.

☐ **Chapter 4: From What and Why to How.** To grow your business, plan to spend 9-15% of your budget on marketing.

☐ **Chapter 5: Website User Experience and Content.** It's important that Google finds your website, but ultimately your website isn't made for Google; it's made for people. To make sure your potential customers have a good experience on your site, it needs to be mobile responsive, full of meaningful content, and offer clear calls to action.

☐ **Chapter 6: Boosting Organic Search.** Without spending any money, it's possible to improve your site's SERP rank through GMB, reviews, and some intentional SEO work on keywords, HTML, images, backlinks, structured data, and security.

☐ **Chapter 7: Boosting Paid Search.** Landing at or near the top of the SERP will require a combination of free and paid strategies. Google Ads are an affordable and effective way to gain traction immediately.

☐ **Chapter 8: Social Media.** Although social media won't bring you quick, qualified leads, it's still massively important to have a solid social presence. Use these channels to engage with people and add value to people's lives—not to sell your shop.

☐ **Chapter 9: Reputation Management.** Nine out of 10 people say they're influenced by positive online reviews when they make purchasing decisions. It's worth the effort, then, to manage your online reputation by asking for and responding to reviews. Every one of them. Every time.

☐ **Chapter 10: Assessment.** Unless you want to waste a bunch of money, you simply can't take a set-it-and-forget-it approach to your digital marketing. Set goals, choose metrics (including CAC!), assess progress, make adjustments, repeat.

Where Digital Marketing's Going

So, that's what we know today—in mid-2018. Things will be slightly different tomorrow. Things will be radically different next year. (Things have changed while I was working on this book, for crying out loud.) It's a bit cliché, but it's true: **The only constant is change.** If you want to stay ahead of your competitors, you'll need to kill them on customer service and stay three steps ahead with your digital marketing strategy. Here are three things to keep an eye on.

Artificial Intelligence

The most pressing development to contend with in the digital marketing space is artificial intelligence (AI) and smart devices. Predictive search is getting smarter and smarter. Advertising is becoming more cleverly targeted. And, perhaps most importantly, speech and text recognition is a real thing, and it has a name: *conversational commerce.* You can make purchases through Facebook, ask Google Assistant to find you a landscaper, and tell Alexa to order you an Uber.

That's all pretty cool, but it's also crazy powerful and it takes digital marketing to entirely new levels:

- ☐ Is your website optimized for voice search?

- ☐ Have you considered the reality that you might be marketing to someone's smart device first—and to the owner of that smart device second?

- ☐ What if your website could deliver personalized content based on what AI knows about each site visitor?

- ☐ Given content's role in effective digital marketing, how great would it be if AI could create and deliver your content automagically?

Build Systems

As you've heard me preach in this book, there are several things you can do to make sure you're getting the most bang for your marketing buck. But with so many tasks to manage, it's easy to get stuck wasting time on things that don't matter. It's important that you build a system into your marketing to make sure you don't allow the tyranny of the urgent to take over.

This doesn't apply just to marketing, by the way. It's relevant to all aspects of your business. Build systems for how you answer the phones, train techs, stock your vans, and more. The more your processes work well, the more you can focus on profitability.

Keep Your Customer First

Keeping your customer first is fundamental to helping your company exist one, five, and even 10 years into the future. The business landscape is littered with the corpses of businesses—and not just HVAC and plumbing shops—that forgot that their customers are the only reason they exist.

Case in point: Back in the early 1980s, British Airways was a government-owned airline that suffered from an awful reputation with customer service, losses up to a staggering *half billion dollars,* and employees who were very good at doing their jobs the very wrong way (sounds like a true government job, right?). Yet, in less than a decade they were able to renew their focus on their customers, overhaul everything from their uniforms to their employee training programs, and became one of the most valuable companies in the world before 1990.

Forget your customers, and your business will struggle. *Focus* on your customers, and your business can thrive. Of course, as time marches on and technology brings us new and better ways to connect with our customers, we have to remember that *people* are changing, too.

Recognizing just how quickly marketing has changed and how the pace of that change is accelerating, it's tough to imagine staying on top of it all as a small business owner. Maybe *you* shouldn't. Maybe, instead, you should let someone else do it for you. In the next chapter, I'll give you some quick thoughts on how to develop a marketing team.

YOUR NEXT STEPS

- ❏ Forget 2025. Is your company accessible by 2018 standards: website, Google Search placement, Google Local Services, chatbots, and more? Are you leveraging current technologies?

- ❏ Technology is always changing. Are you budgeting for major overhauls on your website every two or three years?

- ❏ Are you encouraging your team to experiment with new ways to connect with customers? From on-the-job videos for DIYers to Instagram TV (IGTV), are you looking for ways to try new things?

- ❏ What are five things you're doing now that your biggest competitor isn't even thinking about?

- ❏ What are five things you're doing now that you should never do again?

CHAPTER 12:
GETTING HELP

People tend to have one of four reactions after reading a book like this one:

1. **Awesomesauce.** Now I know exactly what I need to do and how to do it. I can't wait to get started.

2. **This is *way* more involved than I thought it would be.** I understand most of it, but I still have a lot of questions.

3. **Ummm… what?** Can you start all over, please? And go slower this time?

4. **This is a bunch of hooey.** I'm calling my Yellow Pages rep just like I do every year.

If you're in the first camp: Hooray! I'm glad you found this book so helpful and I wish you overwhelming success as you try out new ways to reach new customers. **If you're in the last camp,** and I mean this with not even a tiny bit of sarcasm: You must run the best dang plumber or HVAC shop in the country if the YP is working for you. I hope your business continues to thrive! (But maybe keep this book for future reference.)

As for the folks in the middle: I get it. I do digital marketing for a living, and even I have days when I feel like I'm drowning in data, information, and must-dos. Here's the reality: It's tough to keep a business running—any business—while simultaneously trying to grow it. Quite frankly, even if you had all the skills, you don't have time to be a marketing expert. You're too busy being an HVAC or plumbing expert.

You should get some help.

Getting Help with Your Digital Marketing

If it's true that you, personally, can't manage your marketing on your own (and it is), you have three options for getting help: put a marketing person on your payroll, outsource to a marketing agency, or do both.

Hiring

If you're a large plumbing or HVAC shop with a sizable marketing budget, it's probably worth considering hiring a full-time marketing director. Just brace yourself for a bit of sticker shock. In the United States, the average marketing director earns nearly $136,000 per year—not including benefits—and digital marketing directors earn several thousands more.[1] Of course, that varies depending on things like geographical location, experience, and certifications, but even if you opt to hire a marketing "assistant," you'd need to budget more than $40,000.

While it's costly to hire an in-house marketing director, there is a definite advantage to having someone whose sole job it is to grow your customer base. Still, this approach is rarely the most beneficial for HVAC and plumbing companies.

Outsourcing

Just like different plumbing and HVAC shops have different fees, so do marketing shops. In general, though, you can expect to pay a good agency about 15% of your marketing budget. That means if you have a $125,000 marketing budget, you'll spend just shy of $20,000 for the agency's work. That's a lot of money, for sure, but it's far less money than hiring someone.

If you plan to outsource, try to find someone who specializes in marketing HVAC and plumbing shops. Why? Because they won't have to reinvent the wheel for you, which means they can on-board you quicker. They'll have a proven process, and they don't have to waste much time trying to "figure out" if something's going to work or not. *It just works.*

There are other advantages to outsourcing:

- ☐ **Team approach.** By going with a marketing company, you're not relying on one person's expertise; rather, there's a team of people looking after your account.

- ☐ **Resources.** Marketing companies have access to data, tools, and training an in-house marketer wouldn't—unless you're willing to pay the subscription fees.

- ☐ **Scalability.** Hiring a marketing company allows you to scale your investment as needed. In other words, rather than paying someone the same full-time salary throughout the year, you can put an agency on retainer and only spend what's necessary for a particular time period.

- ☐ **Perspective.** It's helpful to have an outside perspective on your marketing. As business owners, we're too close to our own services, and we forget what it's like to be a customer who's hearing about us for the first time.

- ☐ **Human resources.** While you'll need to do your homework before hiring a marketing company, you won't have the ongoing HR headaches that come with an in-house employee.

The Best of Both Worlds

Most HVAC and plumbing companies can benefit from a both/and approach: Handle in-house the things you feel confident dealing with and outsource everything else.

For example, hire a part-time person to do the creative and front-facing bits of your marketing, but let a marketing company handle the back-end SEO. Or if you have the resources to bring on a tech-oriented person, hire out your social media instead. Or pay a marketing company to build a strategy for you, and then hire someone to implement it. There are no "right" or "perfect" answers here—other than saying "yes" to getting some kind of help.

What to Look for in a Marketing Company

If you decide to engage a company to help with all or part of your marketing, you'll have no shortage of options. Here's what to look for:

- ☐ **Expertise.** I know: *"Duh."* But you're going to be tempted to look first at cost, and I don't want you to make that mistake. First and foremost, you need a marketing company that knows what it's doing. More specifically, look for one that has experience working with the home services industry. Plenty of marketers can help people sell widgets; far fewer understand the nuances of effectively marketing HVAC and plumbing services. How can you tell if you're talking with an expert? Google them. Are they providing thought leadership in the marketing space? Do they share meaningful content on a blog and through their social channels?

- ☐ **Execution.** Look for a marketing company that's actually practicing what it preaches. Don't hire someone on the second page of the SERP with crickets for a social presence and a website that won't pull up on your phone. And don't be shy about asking for data. If someone's calling themselves an SEO expert, ask about their own strategy, investment, and ROI.

- ☐ **Reviews.** This is another "duh," but don't hire a company with poor reviews—or no reviews. And be sure to read a handful of the negative reviews and see how the company responded. Why? Because that's likely how they'll respond to *your* negative reviews.

- ☐ **Accessibility.** Marketing companies have multiple clients, but you should find one that makes you feel like you are their top priority. If they seem to rush through your initial contact, start quoting fees right away, or won't commit to reasonable timeframes, look elsewhere.

☐ **Location.** Keep in mind that accessibility doesn't mean "in your town." Digital communication makes remote partnerships a breeze.

☐ **Chemistry.** You need to *like* your marketing agency. Competence is important, of course, but chemistry is *huge* in a collaborative partnership. Find a marketing company that's curious about you and your business and seems to genuinely care about helping you grow.

YOUR NEXT STEPS

❏ Pull out a piece of paper and create two columns. Label one "things we're already doing" and the other "things we should be doing." Circle the tactics you feel comfortable tackling on your own. (Be honest with yourself about how much skill and time you have to do those things.) Decide how you'll handle the rest—either by hiring someone or by outsourcing.

APPENDIX:
A GLOSSARY OF
DIGITAL MARKETING TERMS

Just like your plumbing and HVAC company, digital marketing has its own set of jargon, including lots of acronyms. I've defined many of them here in an attempt to demystify it all and equip you to speak intelligently with your marketing department (whether in-house or someone to whom you outsource work).

More importantly, I want you to understand these common words and phrases so you're not completely relying on someone else to tell you how things are going and how much it's costing you. If you want to know how much you're spending every time someone clicks on your Google Ad (CPC), I want you to feel empowered and equipped to find out yourself. (It's easy when you know the lingo!)

Please do not try to read this appendix from front to back. That'll make you stabby. Instead, use it as a reference guide. I've put all the entries in alphabetical order, rather than grouping them by category, so you can easily search for the specific word or phrase that has you perplexed. Finally, I haven't bothered to include every single digital marketing term here. That would make *anyone* stabby. Instead, I've provided plain-English definitions for the most important terms HVAC and plumbing pros like you should know.

Actions on Page (Social)	Facebook allows you to add direct calls to action (CTA) buttons on your Page, such as "Call Now" and "Learn More." *Actions on Page* tells you how those CTAs are performing.
Ad Rank	*Ad Rank* describes where a PPC ad lands on a SERP. (See those definitions below.)
Brand Positioning	Branding is a big concept. Practically speaking, though, your *brand* is how your company compares against your competitors in the eyes of your customers.
CAC: Customer Acquisition Cost	*CAC* is what it costs you to get one new customer. To figure CAC, divide the total amount of marketing dollars spent over a period of time by the total number of new customers acquired over that same period of time.
COA: Cost of Acquisition	See *CAC*.
Conversion	*Conversion* simply means someone took an action you wanted them to take. To accurately measure conversions, you have to define what you want people to do—and then present people with relevant CTAs. Example: If someone presses/touches the "Call now" button on your website, that's a conversion. So is entering their email address on a form or downloading a coupon. And, of course, so is scheduling a service call. However, do not make the mistake of assuming each conversion results in a customer for you.
CPC: Cost Per Click	*CPC* is the average amount you pay, per click, in a PPC campaign. While you set your overall PPC budget, Google decides on the actual cost per click, based on a fancy formula *($.01 + your competitor Ad Rank divided by your Quality Score)* and the type of bid strategy your choose to execute.
CPM: Cost Per Thousand	Often, the cost of an ad campaign is expressed in *CPM*- the price you pay for 1,000 impressions. You'll see CPM most often in regard to mass marketing tactics like billboards. (Fun fact: M is the roman numeral for 1,000.)

CTR: **Clickthrough Rate**	Your *CTR* tells you the percentage of people who moved (clicked through) from one step in your marketing strategy to the next. Example: If 7,500 people saw your Facebook ad and 150 of them clicked on it, your CTR for that ad is 2%.
Data: Aggregated	Since you're engaged in omni-channel marketing, you'll need to *aggregate*, or collect, customer data across all of those channels. Example: Measure your COA across all of your marketing efforts combined, not just by looking at your leads' Google Ads CPC.
Domain Authority	*Domain authority* is how authoritative Google believes your entire website (domain) to be, based on a mix of off-site SEO signals like backlinks, social triggers, and reputation factors.
Dwell Time	The amount of time someone hangs out on your website is called *dwell time*. This metric is important because—well, because Google says it is. When people spend time browsing your site, that tells Google you have meaningful, interesting content—which makes it more likely that Google will share your site with other people.
Engagements (Social)	In social media world, *engagements* measures how customers are interacting with your content, e.g., liking your Facebook Page, commenting on a Twitter post, or sharing your YouTube video.
Frequency	*Frequency* is the number of times one person experiences your marketing message. (Not to be confused with *reach*. See below.)
Hyperlocal	*Hyperlocal* describes your ability to locate target customers around your immediate area versus a much larger radius.

Impressions	*Impressions* refers to the number of times something is "served" to consumers. Unlike *reach* (see below), it's the total number of times your content is shown to anyone—and multiple viewings by the same person "count." Example: A plumber purchased a display ad on the Chamber of Commerce website. John visited the site and saw the ad. That's one impression. If John closes out of the site and returns to it, even if he does so immediately, that's another impression.
Keyword	*Keyword* is marketing speak for "words or phrases people search for." Keywords are a significant part of SEO.
Keyword Density	*Keyword density* is the number of times a keyword appears on a page relative to the total word count. It's natural to assume that a higher keyword density would lead to better results, but the opposite is true. When keyword density creeps up, Google gets nervous about spam, so it actually decreases the site's position on SERPs. Example: If the word toilet appears 12 times on a page with 150 words, the keyword density is 8%. Google would definitely frown on this. It prefers keyword densities of 1-3%.
Keyword Frequency	*Keyword frequency* is a simple count of the number of times a keyword appears on a page. This is a much less useful metric than keyword density.
Keyword Prominence	In Googleville, keywords are king, and *keyword prominence* refers to exactly where those words are used on a page: page header, meta tag, beginning of a paragraph, and so on. Keywords in a header indicate to Google that it's likely a page is relevant to someone's query.

Keyword Proximity

Sometimes, people will search for a phrase that matches exactly a phrase on your website—but not often. *Keyword proximity* describes the distance between individual keywords in the search phrase compared to those same keywords on your website. The shorter the distance, the more relevant your site will appear to the Google search.

Example: Let's say someone searches "leak plumber Tulsa" and you have the following header on your website: "Have a clogged drain or pipe with a leak? Call the most trusted plumber in Tulsa!" The keyword proximity between leak and plumber is four; between plumber and Tulsa it's one.

Landing Page

A *landing page* is where a customer "lands" when they click on a link.

A landing page is probably not your home page. It's a page that's built specifically for a marketing campaign. In other words, it's the place where your paid traffic "lands." A great landing page isn't designed to rank on Google search via SEO. Instead, it's designed to convert paid traffic to engage in one, specific action. There are several types of landing page concepts, but we don't need to address them here. Just know they have a specific job, and one job only.

Lookalike Audiences

Lookalike audiences is a Facebook ads feature that allows you to reach new customers who are similar to your current ones. It's one of the more powerful features of Facebook that lets you fine-tune your audience for targeted ads.

Loyalty

A good digital marketing strategy will work to keep current customers and not just gain new ones. We call this *loyalty*. Fun fact: It is three times cheaper to keep a current customer happy and on the books than it is to create a new customer every time.

Map Pack or 3-Pack	When someone searches for a local service or company (or uses a keyword Google thinks is associated with such), Google groups three results together in a *map pack* or *3-pack*. Needless to say, the map pack is a coveted spot on the SERP. Note: Sometimes, there's a fourth listing in the map pack based on Google Ads activity. This section is always being experimented with by Google.
Organic (Traffic)	When people land on your website through a search engine, and they didn't click on an ad to get there, they're considered *organic traffic*. Good SEO will boost your organic traffic, which is free (other than what you invest to get help from someone who knows SEO). It takes *time* to build up organic traffic.
Paid (Traffic)	*Paid traffic* is exactly what it sounds like: people who find themselves on your website because they clicked on an advertisement. It takes *money* to build up paid traffic.
PPC: Pay Per Click	In *PPC* advertising, companies pay a certain amount of money every time someone clicks on their ad. Here's how it works: A company selects some keywords, sets a budget, and creates an ad. When potential customers use any of those same keywords in their search, the PPC ad will show up on the SERP. PPC ads can either have a set price per click, or they can be based on a bid system in which companies compete against other companies using the same keywords.
Quality Score	Your *Quality Score* affects CPC, and Google assigns it based on your keywords and on your PPC ad effectiveness and history. As with all things Google, boosting your Quality Score is complex, but a thoughtful SEM approach will help.

Reach	The total number of people you "touch" with a marketing message is your *reach*. This is different from *frequency*, which is how many times each of those people sees your message. It's also different from *impressions*, which is the total number of times your message is seen (including people who see the same message multiple times). Example: Door hangers can have as high a reach as you want them to. Blanket a couple of subdivisions or an entire community, if you'd like. But, unless they're combined with another tactic, door hangers have terrible frequency. Homeowners see your message once. Given that people need to encounter your message at least seven times before actually paying attention, a one-and-done tactic isn't going to cut it.
Referral (Traffic)	Traffic that comes to your website from sources other than search engines and ads is called *referral traffic*. Examples: Backlinks will show up on Google Analytics as referrals. So will inbound clicks from social media accounts.
Referral (Channel)	People in your *referral channel* are loyal to your business to the point they recommend you to someone else. Referral customers will convert at roughly 1:1.
ROI: Return on Investment	*ROI* tells you the benefit you receive from something relative to its cost. It's an important metric, but because it's typically measured per item or service, it's incomplete. CAC offers a more comprehensive look at how your marketing investments are performing.
SEM: Search Engine Marketing	*SEM* is the overarching term that describes any intentional effort you make to boost your SERP ranking. A good portion of SEM involves paid advertising—approximately 80 billion dollars by 2020.

SEO: Search Engine Optimization	*SEO* is the organic (read: less costly but more time-consuming) arm of SEM. By manipulating your site's content and architecture to be more visible to search engines, you leverage the power of PPC ads.
SERP: Search Engine Results Page	When a prospective customer types a word, phrase, or question into a search engine, the list the search engine displays is called the *SERP*. CTRs decrease dramatically the lower a site is on the SERP, with position number one getting 30% of the clicks and 91.5% of clicks going to first-page results. All sorts of factors determine where your website will land on a SERP, many of which you can manipulate with a smart digital marketing plan.
Sessions	In Google Analytics, a *session* is a group of actions a person (or user) takes on your website at a particular time. For example, someone might come to your homepage, visit your preventive maintenance plan page, bop over to "about," and then hit the "schedule service" button. Collectively, those actions happened in one session on your site. If they close out of your site and come back to it later, that will begin a new session.
SSL: Secure Sockets Layer	*SSL* is a fancy security feature that lets your website address have the "HTTPS" instead of the "HTTP." It may not sound like a huge deal, but Google penalizes in the SERP websites without SSL.
Unique Visitors	A *unique visitor* to your site, now called a user by Google, is one person who comes to your website. If someone visits your site multiple times, they're still only counted as one unique visitor/user.
Views (Social)	Like impressions, *views* indicates the number of times a social post or page is seen. Note that one person may view something multiple times—and all of those views "count."
(Website) Users	See *unique visitors*.

AFTERWORD

I hope this book has been helpful. I hope you've been challenged. I hope you've learned something. But above all, I hope you feel equipped to make smart decisions for your company that can take you to the next level, maximize your lead flow, and, ultimately, make you more money.

This is what I do for a living—help plumbing and HVAC shops do their digital marketing better so they can grow their business and make more money. I'd be honored to have a conversation with you about your shop. The first call's on me. Get started at **dpmarketing.services/bookworm.**

ENDNOTES

Chapter 1

1 https://www.forbes.com/sites/forrester/2017/01/26/us-digital-marketing-spend-will-near-120-billion-by-2021/#42cd9eb6278b

2 https://www.technologyreview.com/the-download/610045/the-average-american-spends-24-hours-a-week-online/

3 https://www.cjr.org/special_report/print_analog_comeback.php/

4 https://www.history.com/news/who-invented-the-internet

5 Ibid.

6 https://livinginternet.com/i/ii_licklider.htm

7 *Inventing the Internet* by Janet Abbate

8 https://www.history.com/news/who-invented-the-internet

9 Ibid.

10 https://webfoundation.org/about/vision/history-of-the-web/

11 https://www.forconstructionpros.com/business/business-services/article/12006782/10-reasons-why-contractors-fail

12 http://blog.needls.com/history-of-advertising/

13 https://www.snopes.com/about-snopes/

14 https://www.npr.org/2018/06/25/623231337/fake-news-an-origin-story

15 https://www.brightlocal.com/learn/local-consumer-review-survey/#Q11

16 https://www.inc.com/craig-bloem/84-percent-of-people-trust-online-reviews-as-much-.html

17 https://conversionxl.com/blog/9-things-to-know-about-influencing-purchasing-decisions/

18 https://www.vendasta.com/blog/50-stats-you-need-to-know-about-online-reviews

19 https://techcrunch.com/2008/09/03/six-degrees-of-separation-is-now-three/

20 https://www.brightlocal.com/learn/local-consumer-review-survey/#Q15

21 https://www.kff.org/other/state-indicator/distribution-by-age/?currentTimeframe=0&selectedRows=%7B%22wrapups%22:%7B%22united-states%22:%7B%7D%7D%7D&sortModel=%7B%22colId%22:%22Adults%2019--25%22,%22sort%22:%22desc%22%7D

22 http://www.pewinternet.org/fact-sheet/internet-broadband/

23 https://www.statista.com/topics/1001/google/

24 http://digitalmarketingmagazine.co.uk/articles/consumers-are-overwhelmed-by-the-pace-of-digital-change

25 Kotler, P., Kartajaya, H., & Setiawan, I. (2016) *Marketing 4.0: Moving from Traditional to Digital*. Hoboken, NJ: John Wiley & Sons, Inc. (pp. 10-11)

Chapter 2

1 https://www.bls.gov/bdm/entrepreneurship/bdm_chart3.htm

2 https://www.statisticbrain.com/startup-failure-by-industry/

3 https://conversionxl.com/blog/9-things-to-know-about-influencing-purchasing-decisions/

4 https://www.guided-selling.org/8-emotional-states-that-influence-purchase-decisions/

5 https://www.invespcro.com/blog/customer-acquisition-retention/

6 Weber, L. & Henderson, L.L. (2014) *The Digital Marketer: Ten New Skills You Must Learn to Stay Relevant and Customer-Centric.* Hoboken, NJ: John Wiley & Sons, Inc. (p. 27)

7 Kotler, P., Kartajaya, H., & Setiawan, I. (2016) *Marketing 4.0: Moving from Traditional to Digital.* Hoboken, NJ: John Wiley & Sons, Inc. (p. 113)

Chapter 3

1 https://www.forbes.com/sites/forbesagencycouncil/2017/08/25/finding-brand-success-in-the-digital-world/#5b261ed4626e

2 http://www.sciencemag.org/news/2011/01/hugs-follow-3-second-rule

3 Kotler, 121

4 https://contentmarketinginstitute.com/2016/07/history-content-marketing/

5 https://www.fastcompany.com/3068820/a-shocking-number-of-people-still-use-their-phone-primarily-to-make-actual-phone-calls

6 http://www.edigitalresearch.cowww.edigitalresearch.com/pdf/sample-benchmarks/Customer%20Service%20Benchmark%20March%202014.pdf

7 https://chatbotsmagazine.com/chatbots-will-redefine-the-conversion-funnel-of-companies-47a286dae9ef

8 https://techcrunch.com/2017/11/07/facebook-introduces-a-messenger-plugin-for-business-websites/

9 https://adespresso.com/blog/facebook-messenger-for-business/

Chapter 4

1 https://www.webstrategiesinc.com/blog/how-much-budget-for-online-marketing-in-2014#Channels

Chapter 5

1 https://www.nngroup.com/articles/how-long-do-users-stay-on-web-pages/

2 https://www.statista.com/statistics/277125/share-of-website-traffic-coming-from-mobile-devices/

3 https://www.forbes.com/sites/ajagrawal/2017/01/06/why-google-hates-your-website-and-how-you-can-fix-it/#6e9c626812d2

4 https://moz.com/blog/mobile-first-indexing-seo

5 https://www.seroundtable.com/google-read-your-web-page-content-out-loud-23413.html

6 https://contentmarketinginstitute.com/what-is-content-marketing/

Chapter 6

1 https://www.smartinsights.com/search-engine-marketing/search-engine-statistics/

2 https://kinsta.com/blog/optimize-images-for-web/

3 https://developers.google.com/web/fundamentals/performance/optimizing-content-efficiency/image-optimization#image_optimization_checklist

4 https://searchenginewatch.com/2017/11/09/image-optimization-101-how-to-rank-higher-in-image-search/

5 https://backlinko.com/search-engine-ranking

6 https://blog.monitorbacklinks.com/seo/types-backlinks-violating-googles-guideliness/

7 http://gs.statcounter.com/browser-market-share/desktop/united-states-of-america

Chapter 7

1 http://www.internetlivestats.com/google-search-statistics/

2 http://www.internetlivestats.com/total-number-of-websites/

Chapter 8

1 https://www.statista.com/statistics/273476/percentage-of-us-population-with-a-social-network-profile/

2 http://www.pewinternet.org/2018/03/01/social-media-use-in-2018/

3 https://www.adweek.com/digital/mediakix-time-spent-social-media-infographic/

4 https://marketingland.com/survey-customers-more-frustrated-by-how-long-it-takes-to-resolve-a-customer-service-issue-than-the-resolution-38756

5 https://www.inc.com/craig-bloem/84-percent-of-people-trust-online-reviews-as-much-.html

6 https://www.forbes.com/sites/ups/2013/08/08/why-businesses-should-listen-to-customers-on-social-media/#773088246153

7 https://hbr.org/2018/01/how-customer-service-can-turn-angry-customers-into-loyal-ones

8 https://coschedule.com/blog/how-often-to-post-on-social-media/

9 https://www.entrepreneur.com/article/303645

10 https://en.wikipedia.org/wiki/List_of_social_networking_websites

11 All from https://blog.hootsuite.com/facebook-demographics/ unless otherwise noted.

12 https://www.statista.com/statistics/266879/facebook-users-in-the-us-by-gender/

13 https://blog.hootsuite.com/youtube-stats-marketers/

14 http://www.pewinternet.org/2018/03/01/social-media-use-in-2018/

15 https://www.statista.com/statistics/296227/us-youtube-reach-age-gender/

16 https://www.forbes.com/sites/meganhills1/2018/03/23/social-media-demographics/#114e3f4783ad

17 All from https://blog.hootsuite.com/instagram-statistics/ unless otherwise noted.

18 https://blog.hootsuite.com/instagram-statistics/

19 All data from https://blog.hootsuite.com/twitter-statistics/ unless otherwise noted.

20 http://www.pewinternet.org/fact-sheet/social-media/

21 https://www.statista.com/statistics/192703/age-distribution-of-users-on-twitter-in-the-united-states/

22 https://www.statista.com/statistics/678794/united-states-twitter-gender-distribution/

23 https://mashable.com/2014/02/04/facebook-men-and-women/#SxHOivgc.uqb

24 https://www.fastcompany.com/3022301/7-powerful-facebook-statistics-you-should-know-about

25 https://www.dreamgrow.com/21-social-media-marketing-statistics/

26 All frequency information except YouTube is from https://coschedule.com/blog/how-often-to-post-on-social-media/

27 All time information except YouTube is from https://sproutsocial.com/insights/best-times-to-post-on-social-media/

28 https://www.oberlo.com/blog/best-time-post-social-media

29 https://blog.hootsuite.com/best-time-to-post-on-facebook-twitter-instagram

30 https://www.oberlo.com/blog/best-time-post-social-media

Chapter 9

1 https://marketingland.com/survey-customers-more-frustrated-by-how-long-it-takes-to-resolve-a-customer-service-issue-than-the-resolution-38756

2 https://www.forbes.com/sites/forbestechcouncil/2018/04/11/online-reviews-are-the-best-thing-that-ever-happened-to-small-businesses/#3c9722df740a

3 https://searchengineland.com/87-percent-customers-wont-consider-low-ratings-228607

4 Ibid.

5 https://www.inc.com/craig-bloem/84-percent-of-people-trust-online-reviews-as-much-.html

6 Kotler, 61.

7 https://www.reviewtrackers.com/online-reviews-survey/

8 https://www.vendasta.com/blog/50-stats-you-need-to-know-about-online-reviews

9 https://www.statista.com/statistics/307050/online-adults-posting-product-or-brand-reviews-on-the-internet-by-generation/

10 https://www.reviewtrackers.com/online-reviews-survey/

11 https://www.inc.com/andrew-thomas/the-hidden-ratio-that-could-make-or-break-your-company.html

12 https://www.brightlocal.com/learn/local-consumer-review-survey/#Q13

13 https://fitsmallbusiness.com/how-to-use-angies-list/

14 https://www.reviewtrackers.com/online-reviews-survey/

15 https://www.brightlocal.com/learn/local-consumer-review-survey/

16 https://www.reviewtrackers.com/online-reviews-survey/

17 https://www.inc.com/visa/don%C3%A2%E2%82%AC%E2%84%A2t-fear-a-complaining-customer.html

18 https://www.forbes.com/sites/amymorin/2014/05/06/why-negative-reviews-can-be-good-for-business/#36d-7856829fa

Chapter 12

1 https://www1.salary.com/Marketing-Director-Salary.html

Appendix

Made in the USA
Coppell, TX
23 December 2020